E

BIBLE BASED PRAYERS AND PRAISE

Clarice Bell Church

ISBN: 978-0-9991050-5-4

CONTENTS

INTRODUCTION

I T IS MY prayer that this book will be used as a guide for the reader to use the words of the Bible to pray that which is true, based on the Word of God (the Holy Bible). God wants us to say and pray with faith, what He says in His Word. Romans 10:9 states "If you confess with your mouth the Lord Jesus and believe in your heart that God has raised Him from the dead You will be saved". Note that this scripture tells us to confess with your mouth, in other words, speak and believe in our heart, and it shall be done; it will be manifested in Christ Jesus.

As believers or as one seeking to make Jesus Christ your Lord and Savior, we must remember to always pray and not lose heart (Luke 18:1). When we continually pray, praise and seek God in faith, we please God and He will never leave us nor forsake us.

It is important to pray those things which agree with God's will, His way and His Word. The prayers and praise in this book may be used as part of your daily prayers and praise, and as a guide for praying prayers which include quotes from the Holy Bible, which by faith will come to pass.

You may also study, meditate on and journal your own thoughts and, prayers as you read the scriptures included throughout the writings of The Path To "Bible Based Prayers and Praise".

As you pray and seek the Lord, your faith will increase, which is important because "without faith it is impossible to please Him (God)" (Hebrews 11:6).

Now let the Prayers and Praise begin in Jesus name!

DEDICATION

To my four children: Ava Bell Taylor M.D., Eric Wyatt Bell, Clarice Bell Strayhorn M.D., and Roy Charles Bell Jr. who went to Heaven on April 7, 2011. This book is also, dedicated to my beloved Bishop Dale C. Bronner and my Word of Faith Family Worship Cathedral sisters and brothers.

FOREWORD

PRAYER IS OUR connection and lifeline to God! Prayer is that which enables us to discern the will of God for our lives and serves as the foundation of our ability to understand the Scripture. Prayer precedes revival. If ever there was a time when we need the power of prayer and praise in our life, it is NOW!

E.M. Bounds said, "What the Church needs today is not more machinery or better, not new organizations or more and novel methods, but men whom the Holy Ghost can use—men of prayer, men mighty in prayer." This is not merely specific of men but more generically of mankind to include women.

Powerful things happen when men and women pray and praise. I like to begin my prayers with thanksgiving and praise. Then I like to end my prayers with thanksgiving and praise. Prayer and praise go together. Praise is the evidence that you have faith that God has heard and will answer your prayer.

Prayer and praise are a lifestyle for followers of Christ. Timothy Keller reminds us that, "to pray is to accept that we are, and always will be, wholly dependent on God for everything." I encourage you to use this wonderful resource that Rev. Clarice Church has written to facilitate your prayer life and inspire awesome praise in your heart!

Make prayer and praise a part of your daily routine. Billy Graham reminded us, "True prayer is a way of life, not just for use in cases of emergency. Make it a habit, and when the need arises you will be in practice." Your best days are ahead! Get ready for your life to go to another level of intimacy and power with God our Father.

Bishop Dale C. Bronner, D. Min.
Founder/Senior Pastor
Word of Faith Family Worship Cathedral
Austell, GA

SALVATION

SCRIPTURE REFERENCE

Acts 3:19

19) *Repent therefore and be converted, that your sins may be blotted out, so that times of refreshing may come from the presence of the Lord.*

PRAYER

Father God, I am thankful that when I confessed my sins, repented and made Jesus Christ my Lord and Savior, that You called me out of the darkness of Satan's dominion into Your marvelous light. You have blotted out my sins and I am saved. I thank You for adopting me into the Family of God.

Lord, I shall no longer conform to the ways of the world; I shall obey the Word of God. I shall conform to Your will and Your way. I have been transformed by my faith in Your Son, Jesus Christ, and I renew my mind by studying, and obeying the principles, precepts and commands of the Word of God (the Holy Bible).

Father, although I know You are present within me and around me, I joyfully go to the House of the Lord (the church), where I am refreshed, and where I enjoy Your magnified presence among Your children, the people of God.

Heavenly Father, thank You for saving me and for Your unconditional love. I love You and I give You all the glory, honor and praise in Jesus' name Amen.

SALVATION

Scripture Reference

Acts 4:12

12) *"Nor is there salvation in any other, for there is no other name (than Jesus) under heaven given among men by which we must be saved".*

Prayer

Father God, you did not send Your son into the world to condemn the world, but that the world through Him (Jesus) might be saved (John3:17) Thank You Lord, for not condemning me when I was yet in sin, but instead You gave me the opportunity to be saved. One cannot earn salvation; it is a gift from God (Ephesians 2:8). Father, I know You saved me when I confessed I was a sinner, repented (turned from sin) and asked Jesus to be my Lord and Savior. I am now saved through faith; for that I say thank you.

Dear God, I study Your Word, the Holy Bible, which is my guide and instruction manual on how to live according to Your will.

Great and Wonderful God, may Your Spirit enable me to have the character of Jesus Christ. It is in the precious name of Jesus I pray. Amen.

SALVATION

SCRIPTURE REFERENCE

Acts 5:31-32

31) *Him (Jesus), God has exalted to His right hand to be Prince and Savior, to give repentance.... and Forgiveness of sins.*

32) *And we are His witnesses to these things, and so also is the Holy Spirit whom God has given to those who obey Him.*

PRAYER

Father, thank You for Jesus, Prince Of Peace and my Savior, who paid the price for my sins with His blood. Because of His sacrifice, I was able to accept Jesus as my Lord, repent by turning away from my sins to follow Him and obey the Word of God through the enabling power of the Holy Spirit. Thank You Lord, for giving me the awesome gift of salvation.

Father, I shall not fail to bare witness of Your wonderful work, Your love, Your mercy, Your favor and Your peace that, regardless to circumstances, passes all understanding.

Dear God, because of who You are, I praise You this day and every day of my life. In Jesus' name I pray. Amen.

SALVATION

Scripture Reference

Ephesians 2:4-5

4)   *But God, who is rich in mercy, because of His great love with which He loved us*

5)   *even when we were dead in trespasses, made us alive together with Christ (by grace you have been saved).*

Prayer

Heavenly Father, thank You for Your mercy and Your great love for me. Thank You for loving me even when I was living in sin and did not know You. I was dead, that is, separated from You because of my trespasses. Praise You, Father, that by faith I was saved when I accepted Jesus Christ, (who paid the price for my sins with His own blood) as my Lord and Savior. Whereas, I was lost, I am now reconciled unto God by grace. I am saved by Your mercy and Your favor. So, I say thank You.

Father, lead me in the divine way I should go. Help me to be bold in sharing the good news of Jesus with family, friends and those I meet. Place Your words in my heart and my mouth as I testify of Your good works and Your great love. I love You, praise You and I give You all the glory in the name of Jesus. Amen.

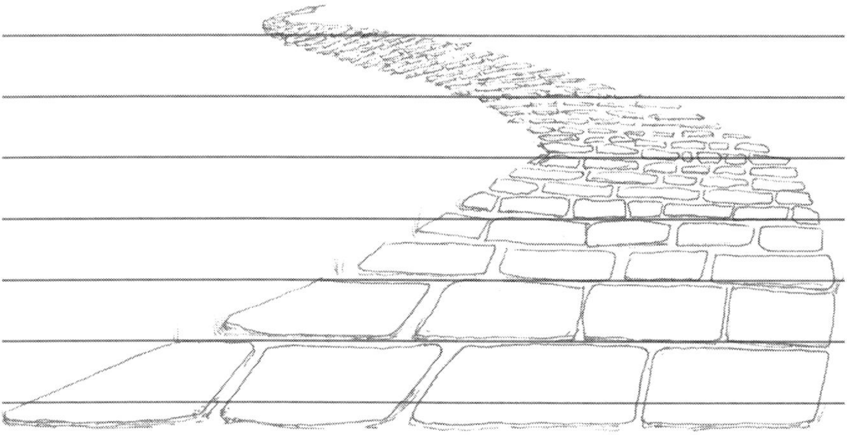

SALVATION

SCRIPTURE REFERENCE

Isaiah 61:10a

10a) I will greatly rejoice in the Lord, my soul shall be joyful in my God; for he has clothed me with the garment of salvation, He has covered me with the robe of righteousness...

PRAYER

Dear God, I rejoice in who You are and in Your goodness each dy. I am joyful because Jesus Christ is my Savior. You have clothed me with the garment of salvation and the robe of righteousness. Because I live by faith, I am justified, just as if I never sinned. Jesus who knew no sin, was made sin on my behalf so that I might be made the righteousness of God (2 Corinthians 5:21). So, I say thank You.

Thank You God for saying You will never leave me nor forsake me. I know You are present and, in Your presence, there is fullness of joy. When I think of losing a loved one and become sad, I think of Your love for me and my tears of sadness are replaced by tears of joy.

Father, You are the source of my joy. You are the source of my salvation; You are the source of my righteousness and every other good and perfect gift.

Thank You Father for Your forgiveness, mercy, favor, protection and most of all I thank You for Your Unconditional Love. It is in the name of Your Precious Son Jesus I pray. Amen.

SALVATION

SCRIPTURE REFERENCE

Matthew 10:22b

22)   …He who endures to the end will be saved.

PRAYER

Heavenly Father, thank You for sending Your Son Jesus to earth, not to condemn the world, but that by receiving Jesus as Lord and Savior, mankind will be saved from hell and adopted into the family of God.

Thank You for saving me. There is no greater gift than that of salvation. My trust is in You, the living God.

Father, through the power of the Holy Spirit within me, help me to live in the spirit and not the flesh. I shall feed my spirit with the Word of God. By obeying the Word, I shall develop the character of Christ Jesus. When Satan tempts me to sin, I shall submit to God, "resist the devil and he will flee from (me)". (James 4:7).

Dear God, fill me again with the Holy Spirit and continue to enable me to endure to the end that I may fulfill the purpose for which I was created. I declare and decree I am saved and I shall reach my destiny in the name of Jesus. Amen.

SALVATION

Matthew 22:14

14) "For many are called, but few are chosen".

PRAYER

Father, when You called me, I surrendered my life and became totally committed to You: heart, mind, body, spirit and soul through Christ Jesus. Thank You for choosing me and adopting me into the Family of God. I am now a member of Your chosen generation. I am now a child of God, and You are my Father. You are my Heavenly Daddy. You call me beloved, the apple of Your eye and Your friend. So, I say thank you.

Father, I know that faith without works is dead. Therefore, I shall work as unto the Lord and diligently serve the Kingdom of God. My heart yearns to live according to Your perfect will each day of my life. Your Word is a lamp to my feet, (Psalm 119:105). My steps are ordered by the Lord and You delight in my way, (Psalm 37:23).

Dear God, thank You for including me as one of Your chosen. Please continue to order my steps in Your Word in Jesus' name. Amen.

SALVATION

John 3:16

16) For God so loved the world that He gave His only begotten Son, that whoever believes in Him should not perish but have everlasting life.

PRAYER

Dear God, today I just want to thank You for Jesus. I thank You for the birth, death and resurrection of Jesus.

Thank You Father God, for loving me so much that You gave Your only begotten Son, Jesus, to shed His innocent blood to pay the price for my sins. Thank You that it is because of what Jesus did, I can confess my sins, accept Jesus as my Lord, obey the Word of God, and I will receive everlasting life. I thank You for my Savior, Jesus Christ.

I am thankful that by faith I am no longer separated from You, (You are in me) and I shall spend eternity with You in heaven and occupy one of the heavenly mansions You have prepared for the children of God.

Lord, I entreat You to rebuke Satan on my behalf and I will resist the Devil and he shall surely flee. Lord, I pray that peace, harmony and love will prevail in my family and in the families of all the children of God.

Father, pour out You Spirit upon me and my loved ones. Fill us with the Holy Spirit. I thank You for Your favor upon my life and upon all the people of God. It is in Jesus name I pray. Amen.

21

SALVATION

SCRIPTURE REFERENCE

John 8:31-32

31)   ..." If you abide in My word, you are My disciples indeed.

32)   And you shall know the truth and the truth shall make you free".

PRAYER

Father, Your Word is the source by which I know the truth, although, the fact is sometimes I feel sick, the truth is: by speaking God's Word "by His (Jesus) stripes I am healed" my healing is manifested.

When I received Jesus as my Lord and Savior, I became Your disciple. The truth is I am free from worry through Christ Jesus. I have the "peace of God which surpasses all understanding". (Philippians 4:7)

Lord, thank You for being My Savior, My Deliverer, My Hope, My Comforter, My Protector, My Healer and My Provider who meets all my needs. You give me good and perfect gifts. I abide in Your Word, and I use the Word of God (the Bible) as the instruction manual to teach me how I should live.

Father, the truth is, You are the reason I live, for it is in You I "live, move and have my being... (Acts17:28)

Father, because I know the truth, the truth has made me free. I exalt You and I extol You in the name of Jesus. Amen.

GOD OUR PROVIDER

Acts 17:24-25

24) God who made the world and everything in it, since He is Lord of heaven and earth, does not dwell in temples made with hands.

25) …He gives to all life, breath and all things.

PRAYER

Almighty God, who made the world and everything in it, I thank You for forming me and breathing into my nostrils the breath of life so that I became a living being. For creating me, I say "Thank You".

Father God, You are Lord of heaven and earth, and the giver of all good and perfect gifts.

Thank You Heavenly Father, for being my Provider. Thank You for a place to live, food to eat, water to drink and clothes to wear. I shall always be grateful for Your grace favor, mercy, protection, love, abundant blessings and for Jesus Christ who died on the cross to pay for my sins so that I may be saved and have eternal life. I pray in the precious name of Jesus. Amen.

GOD OUR PROVIDER

SCRIPTURE REFERENCE

Acts 17:28

28) For in Him we live and move and have our being, as also some of your own poets have said, 'For we are also His offspring'.

PRAYER

Lord, You are my everything.
In You I live, move and have my being.
You are my everything.
You are my needs met.
On You my heart is set.
You are my everything
The Joy I receive.
In you I believe.
You are my everything.
In the morning I think of You.
And all day long I do too.
With a smile on my face, I confess; for You are my greatest happiness.
You are my savior.
You are my Lord.
I Love You! I love You!
YOU ARE MY EVERYTHING!
YOU ARE MY EVERYTHING!
In the name of Jesus, I pray. Amen!

GOD OUR PROVIDER

SCRIPTURE REFERENCE

1 Chronicles 16:8-9b

8) *Oh, give thanks unto the Lord! Call upon His name, make known His deeds among the peoples.*

9b) *Talk of all His wondrous works!*

PRAYER

Father, I came to give You thanks and to call upon Your name. I thank You not only for what You do for me, but for who You are. You supply all my needs according to Your riches in glory through Christ Jesus.

Lord, I am thankful for Your awesome deeds. You are Jehovah Rapha, the Lord Our Healer. I thank You for healing me each time I was sick. You are Jehovah Shalom, which means the Lord Our Peace. Thank You Father, that when I call on the name of Jesus, that You give me peace that passes all understanding. I declare and decree peace in the name if Christ Jesus regarding jobs, family, finances and relationships. For peace that passes understanding. I say thank you.

Heavenly Father, I call on the name of Jehovah Jireh, our Provider. For Your wonderous work of providing food, clothing, shelter, protection and a sound mind. I say thank You.

Dear God, order my steps in Your Word. Lead me in the way I should go. And let Your will be done in me, to me and through me. I shall show my love for You by obeying your Word through Christ Jesus. It is with thanksgiving I praise You in the name of Jesus. Amen.

GOD OUR PROVIDER

SCRIPTURE REFERENCE

1 Corinthians 2:12

12) *Now we have received, not the spirit of the world, but the Spirit who is from God, that we might know the things that have been freely given to us by God.*

PRAYER

Father, I thank You that I no longer have the spirit of the world, because You have given me the Holy spirit. I no longer conform to the ways of the world, instead, I conform to Your will and Your way.

Father, thank You for revealing the things You have freely given me. You have given me life, and that more abundantly (John 10:10). When I acknowledge You, You guide me and direct my paths (Proverbs 3:6). If I sin, I have an advocate, Jesus, who is the propitiation for my sins (1 John 2:2). Your presence is always with me (Matthew 28:20b). Father, You have given me spiritual and tangible gifts too numerous to describe. All that I have, You gave me.

I thank You Father for who You are and for all the things You have freely given me, in the name of Jesus. Amen.

GOD OUR PROVIDER

SCRIPTURE REFERENCE

2 Corinthians 9:8

8)   *And God is able to make all grace abound toward you, that you,
     always having all sufficiency in all things, may have an abundance
     for every good work.*

PRAYER

Thank You God for giving me abundant grace, that is abundant
favor. Almighty Father, it is because You have blessed me, I am able
to give to the poor and the needy, and to help those who have lost
hope. When I am weak You make me strong.

Father God, thank You for sufficiency in all things; I am grateful.
Thank You for shelter, food and for meeting my every need. Lord,
because You are my Provider, I have abundance for every good
work and I am able to serve mankind according to Your will and
Your purpose.

Lord, for who You are, I give you all the glory, honor and praise
in the name of Jesus. Amen.

GOD OUR PROVIDER

SCRIPTURE REFERENCE

James 1:17

17)	*Every good gift and every perfect gift is from above, and comes down from the Father of lights, with whom there is no variation or shadow of turning.*

PRAYER

Father, I thank You for every good gift and every perfect gift You provide for me and my family each day. I thank You for divine desires: for the desire to serve You and to please You in all I say, think, and do. Thank You for empowering me to exemplify the character of Jesus to my family, friends, neighbors and the world. Thank You for giving me the spirit of a servant, as well as a leader.

Lord, I am available to be used by You. Use me Father. I commit myself to letting Your will be done in my life. Not my will, but Your will be done in me and through me. Thank You Heavenly Father for giving me a blessed and abundant life.

Dear God, I love You. You are my Father, my Lord my King, my Redeemer, my Deliverer, my Provider and my Savior forever and ever. I thank You for the perfect gift of Jesus Christ and it is in His name I pray. Amen.

GOD OUR PROVIDER

Philippians 4:19

19) *And my God shall supply all your need according to His riches in glory by Christ Jesus.*

PRAYER

Lord, I thank You for supplying all my needs, my family's needs financial needs, health needs and my relationship needs. Thank You for being my Provider, my Healer, my Peace, my Deliverer, my Banner of victory and my precious Savior.

Father, 1 John 4:8 states: "God is love" and I know You live in me. Therefore, I have abundant love for all mankind. Father, thank You for giving me the character of Jesus Christ and enabling me to have unwavering love for everyone regardless to who they are, whether sinner or saved by the grace of God. Lord, let Your light shine upon me, in me and through me that You may be glorified.

Dear God, I praise You for being the great "I AM". The "I AM" who becomes my Provider of whatever I need, whenever I need it. For that I say thank You.

Father You, are my Strength. You are my strength to live, to laugh, to love, to learn, and to leave a legacy. I worship You. You are King of kings and Lord of lords. I love You and I thank You for loving me. It is in the precious name of Jesus Christ I pray. Amen.

GOD'S COMMAND

SCRIPTURE REFERENCE

1 Corinthians 6:18-20

18) *Flee sexual immorality. Every sin that a man does is outside the body, but he who commits sexual immorality sins against his own body.*

19) *Or do you not know that your body is the temple of the Holy Spirit who is in you, whom you have from God, and you are not your own?*

20) *For you were bought at a price; therefore, glorify God in your body and in your spirit, which are God's.*

PRAYER

Father, because Jesus paid the price for my salvation: my body, soul and spirit belong to You. I am not my own. Thank You for making my body the temple of the Holy Spirit.

Thank You Father, because of my faith: You have received me as an heir to the kingdom of God and joint heir with Jesus Christ.

Father, "in the beginning was the Word, and the Word was with God and the Word was God" (John 1:1). Father, You are the Creator of the universe, and not only were You the Word in the beginning, but You are the Word now and forevermore.

Lord, I shall avoid sexual immorality and obey all Your commands. I shall diligently seek You, so that I may grow closer to you each day. Father, I magnify Your Holy Name. It is in the name of Jesus' I pray. Amen.

GOD'S COMMAND

SCRIPTURE REFERENCE

1 Corinthians 7:2

2)   *Nevertheless, because of sexual immorality, let each man have his own wife, and let each woman have her own husband.*

PRAYER

All powerful God, deliver me from evil. Father, help me to employ the power of the Holy Spirit within me to deliver me from sexual immorality. Help me to only desire the spouse You choose for me. Keep me from following carnal, ungodly, sinful desires of the flesh, and instead I shall obey the Word of God and follow the Holy Spirit within me. It is my desire to be equally yoked with a person who has made Jesus their Lord and Savior.

Thank You Father, for loving me and delivering me from sexual immorality. Dear God, You are awesome and worthy of all the glory, honor, and praise in Jesus' name. Amen.

GOD'S COMMAND

Deuteronomy 6:5

5) *"You shall love the Lord your God with all your heart, with all your soul and with all your strength".*

PRAYER

Lord, I come this day to express my love for You. I love You with all my heart, soul, mind and strength. I magnify Your name for You are worthy of all the glory, honor and praise.

Thank You Lord for being my Savior. Not only did You save me, redeem me and adopted me into Your family but You also protect me from harm and danger during these perilous times. For that I say thank You.

Father, in Proverbs 15:8, You said "the prayer of the upright is (your) delight". Lord I pray that You find delight in my prayers, praise and my worship, as I worship You in spirit and in truth. I pray that it is Your delight when I obey the Word of God at home, everywhere I go and at all times. Lord because I love You, I want to please You in all that I do, all that I say and all that I think.

Once again, I say I love You with all my heart, with all my soul and with all my strength. I bless Your holy name. In the precious name of Jesus. Amen.

PRAISE THE LORD

SCRIPTURE REFERENCE

Isaiah 12:4

4) *And in that day you will say: "Praise the Lord, call upon His Name; declare His deeds among the peoples, make mention that His name is exalted...*

PRAYER

Lord I praise You. You are worthy of all the glory, honor and praise. You are awesome and greatly to be praised. I exalt Your name. You created the heavens and the earth (Genesis 1:1). You formed man out of the dust of the ground and breathed into his nostrils the breath life: and mankind became a living being (Genesis 2:7).

Thank You Father, that when I call on the name of Jesus, I am safe from harm and danger; I am protected.

Father, I am continually aware that nothing can separate me from Your love. You are with me at all times, and no weapon formed against me shall succeed for I am more than a conqueror through the Lord (Romans 8: 37).

Dear God, I am not ashamed of the gospel of Christ, for it is the power of God to salvation for everyone that believes (Romans 1:16).

Thank You, Father, for salvation, forgiveness, mercy, deliverance and grace. I exalt You. Praise You and I love You. I pray in the name of Jesus. Amen.

PRAISE THE LORD

SCRIPTURE REFERENCE

Isaiah 25:1

1)   *Lord, You are my God. I will exalt You, I will praise Your name, for You have done wonderful things; Your counsels of old are faithfulness and truth.*

PRAYER

Holy, Righteous, Merciful Father, I exalt You; I praise Your Holy name. Thank You for the wonderful things You do.

You woke me up this morning and this is the day You have made, I will rejoice and be glad in it. You have not given (me) a spirit of fear, but of power and of love and of a sound mind (2 Timothy 1:7). Father God, I shall not fear, for You are with me and You shall not forsake me.

The Spirit of Love is with me, because Your Spirit is within my heart, and You are Love. I love every human being regardless to the person's race, color, creed, circumstances or status in life. I love You God with all that I am: mind soil, body, heart, strength and spirit.

There are times when the facts say I am sick, but I know the truth is by Jesus' stripes and by His Blood I am healed. My healing shall be manifested by Christ Jess.

Thank You Lord, it is because You are my Shepherd, I shall not want. You are the Provider of all that I need. I praise You, Father, for who You are, in the name of Jesus. Amen.

PRAISE THE LORD

SCRIPTURE REFERENCE

Psalm 9:1-2

1) *I will praise You, O Lord, with my whole heart; I will tell of all Your marvelous works.*

2) *I will be glad and rejoice in You; I will sing praise to Your name, O Most High.*

PRAYER

Father, I give You the highest praise. I rejoice in You with the song, with the clapping of my hands and with the lifting of my hands in total surrender to Your will.

Most High God, it is in You that I live, move and have my being. Marvelous are Your works. You supply all my needs. When I am sick, You heal me. When I am weak, You become my strength. Marvelous are Your works. When there is trouble all around me, You give me peace. When I think I can't make it, You help me to stand endure and make it through. For that, I say thank You.

Father, marvelous are Your works. Your word is a lamp to my feet and a light to my path. Thank You Father, for providing me with every good gift and every perfect gift. Lord, I wake up each morning with expectancy, because You give me favor and daily benefits.

Father, there is no love greater than Your love, which never changes, even when I am unlovable. So I say thank You. Heavenly Father, I will always be careful to give You all the glory, all the honor, and all the praise in the precious name of Jesus. Amen.

PRAISE THE LORD

SCRIPTURE REFERENCE

Psalm 34: 1, 3

1) *I will bless the Lord at all time; His praise shall continually be in my mouth.*

3) *Oh, magnify the Lord with me, and let us exalt His name together.*

PRAYER

Father, I will bless the Lord at all times. I magnify the name of Jesus. I exalt the name of the Lord Jesus. The adversary may attack my family, my finances, and my relationships, but I know no weapon formed against me shall prosper. Father, I magnify the Lord for interceding on my behalf.

Father, I am thankful because according to Your Word: "the eyes of the Lord are on the righteous and His ears are open to their cry." (Psalms 34:15) Thank You Lord for being mindful of me and for calling me Your friend. Thank You for hearing and answering my prayers.

Father, I thank You for Your grace, Your power, Your mercy, Your miracles, and Your praise is continually in my mouth. Thank You for Jesus in whose name I pray. Amen.

PRAISE THE LORD

SCRIPTURE REFERENCE

Psalm 100:4

4)   *Enter into His gates with thanksgiving, and into His courts with praise. Be Thankful to Him and bless His name.*

PRAYER

Lord, I enter Your gates with thanksgiving and Your courts with praise. Father, I thank You for Your loving kindness. I bless Your Holy name. You are worthy of all the praise.

Dear God, I surrender my will and my ways to You and ask You to let Your will be done in my life. Father, I thank You for giving me favor in the areas of finances, health and relationships.

Father, I praise You for life and the opportunity to proclaim Your greatness, Your love and Your awesome works. I praise You for protecting me from harm and danger: seen and unseen. I thank You for providing all my needs. I thank You for being my Healer and giving me peace regardless to the circumstances. I thank You for blessing my home, my family and friends. Father, I praise You for giving me favor with You and mankind.

Heavenly Father, there are no words in the human language to describe how much I love You. So I simply say, I love You, with all that I am and all that I shall become. In the powerful, and perfect name of Jesus I pray. Amen.

PRAISE THE LORD

SCRIPTURE REFERENCE

Psalm 63:3-4

3) *Because Your lovingkindness is better than life, my lips shall praise You.*

4) *Thus, I will bless You while I live; I will lift up my hands in Your name.*

PRAYER

Thank You Father, for Your lovingkindness. I bless Your holy name. You are worthy of the praise.

Lord, I enter Your gates with thanksgiving and Your courts with praise. You are good to me and Your mercy is everlasting.

Father, I lift my hands without wrath and doubting, and I applaud Your greatness. I surrender my will and ways to You and ask that Your will be done in me as it is done in heaven.

Father, I pray that You open doors of opportunity for the people of God. I Thank You for life and the opportunity to proclaim Your greatness and declare Your awesome works. I thank You for protecting me from harm and danger: seen and unseen, for providing my needs, for saving me and adopting me into the family of God, for blessing my home, my family, and for divine favor with man and God.

Dear God, there are no words in the human language to describe how much I love You. I simply say, I adore You and I love You with all that I am and all that I shall become. In the powerful and perfect name of Jesus I pray. Amen.

PRAISE THE LORD

SCRIPTURE REFERENCE

Psalm 150:2,6

2) *Praise Him for His mighty acts; Praise Him according to His excellent greatness!*

6) *Let everything that has breath praise the Lord.*

PRAYER

Father, I praise You for Your mighty acts in my life: for waking me up this morning and giving me the desire to study the Word of God. I praise You for protecting me from harm and danger. Father, I acknowledged that in the midst of trouble, only You can give me peace. Mighty is Your act of providing those things I have need of. I praise You for opening doors of opportunity and for making my latter days better than my former.

Father, I believe and receive the miracles that are forthcoming in my life. I praise You for blessings and miracles in my life, and in my relationships. I thank You for health and financial blessings. Father, I rebuked the attacks of Satan, and ask You almighty God to continue to rebuke Satan on my behalf.

Lord, as You place those who need to be encouraged on my heart, I will be careful to reach out to them and without delay I will pray. I know, prayer changes things. Father, I continue to offer You the sacrifice of praise for Your never-ending love for me. So, it is with the great love that I say thank You. In Jesus' name. Amen.

GLORY OF GOD

SCRIPTURE REFERENCE

1 Corinthians 10:31b

31b) …whatever you do, do all to the glory of God.

PRAYER

Father God, each day I shall glorify You, honor You, praise You and worship You with my whole heart. Lord, You are awesome! I exalt You and extol You as my King of kings and Lord of lords. Lord, it is my desire to please You in all I say and do (in all my thoughts, all my words and all my deeds).

Father, I shall be careful to speak words which conform with the commands, promises and precepts in the Holy Bible, which is the divine instruction manual for righteous living. Whatever I do, I do as unto God, and to His glory in the name of Jesus Christ. Amen.

PROMISES OF GOD

SCRIPTURE REFERENCE

2 Corinthians 1:20

*20) For all the promises of God in Him are Yes, and in Him Amen, to
the glory of God through us.*

PRAYER

This day Father, I declare Your promises are yes and amen, and
it is done. Father, I declare the Word of God which says: as for me
and my house, we will serve the Lord. I decree when the enemy
comes against me like a storm, I will lift a standard against him; the
standard of Jesus Christ.

Father, I declare peace in my home and peace of mind that
passes all understanding. I declare health in my body; by Jesus'
stripes I am healed. Lord I declare I shall leave a spiritual and
tangible inheritance for my children and grandchildren through
Christ Jesus.

Father, this day I stand in the gap for my natural and spiritual
sons, daughters, relatives, and friends who desperately need You. I
plead the blood of Jesus over them all.

Heavenly Father, I know that whoever confess their sins,
repents and by faith makes Jesus their Lord and Savior, they shall
be saved. It is through faith in Jesus one must receive salvation. It is
in the name of Jesus, I am adopted into the family of God and given
eternal life. For my salvation, dear God, I say thank you.

Lord, I thank You for Your promise of abundant blessings, favor
and mercy. It is in the precious name of Jesus I pray. Amen.

GLORIFY THE LORD

SCRIPTURE REFERENCE

2 Corinthians 4:16

16) *Therefore, we do not lose heart. Even though our outward man is perishing, yet the inward man is being renewed day by day.*

PRAYER

Father God, I shall not lose heart nor be discouraged, although, as I grow older, I sometimes have pains and health issues.

Lord, as long as I live, I shall continue to obey Your covenant and do the work of the Kingdom of God. I shall continue to fulfill the purpose for which You created me.

Father, thank You for renewing my inward man each day. I give You all the glory, all the honor and all the praise. You are wonderful, merciful, almighty and it is through You I live, move and have my being.

Thank You Lord, that "weeping may endure for a night, but joy comes in the morning" (Psalm30:5).

Heavenly Father, You are the source of my joy. You are "my exceeding joy" (Psalm 43:4).

Dear God, You are Lord of lords and King of kings. You are my Provider, the great "I AM", and I thank You for who You are in Jesus' name. Amen

Reconciliation

Scripture Reference

2 Corinthians 5: 17-18

17) *Therefore, if anyone is in Christ, he is a new creation; old things have passed away, behold, all things have become new,*

18) *Now all things are of God, who has reconciled us to Himself through Jesus Christ, and has given us the ministry of reconciliation.*

Prayer

Father, thank You for giving me the ministry of reconciliation. I know You are not willing that any should perish but that all should come to repentance and that is my desire also. Father I ask You to lead me to divine encounters and give me the boldness to express to those I encounter, just how much You love them and how much You desire for them to receive eternal life, by accepting Jesus as their Lord and Savior.

Dear God, I call on the name of Jesus today, the name that is above every name. I look unto Jesus, the author and the finisher of my faith.

Father, I ask that You meet the needs of Your People; financial needs, health needs and relationship needs.

Lord, because 1 John 4:8 states God is love, and I know You live in me, Father help me to have unwavering agape love for all mankind. Father, let Your light shine upon me, in me and through me that You may be glorified.

Heavenly Father, I praise You for being the great "I AM". The "I AM" who becomes whatever I need, when I need it, based on Your infinite knowledge and my obedience. So, I say thank You for Your blessings and Your love. I love You and it is in the precious name of Jesus I pray. Amen.

GOD MY STRENGTH

SCRIPTURE REFERENCE

2 Corinthians 12:9a

9a) *And He (the Lord) said to me, "My grace is sufficient for you, for My strength is made perfect in weakness".*

PRAYER

Dear God, when I feel weak physically or spiritually, I am comforted by Your promise that Your grace is sufficient. When I am weak, Your strength is manifested in me and I am able to let Your will be done to me, in me and through me.

Father God, it is because You love me, and I obey the Word, I continue to live victoriously. Thank You Lord for manifesting, in my life, the promises You made in the Holy Bible.

Almighty God, thank You for giving Your Son, Jesus Christ to pay the price for my sins and who is on Your right continually interceding and rebuking Satan on my behalf. Father, please continue to use me for Your glory. Again, I ask that You let Your will be done to me, in me and through me. Lord, help me to fulfill the purpose for which I was created. For these blessings, I give You all the glory, all the honor and all the praise in the name of Jesus. Amen.

GOD'S COMMANDMENTS

SCRIPTURE REFERENCE

Deuteronomy 6:17-18

17) *You shall diligently keep the commandments of the Lord your God, His testimonies and His statutes which He has commanded you.*

18) *And you shall do what is right and good in the sight of the Lord, that it may be well with you…*

PRAYER

Lord I shall diligently keep Your commandments and what is right and good in Your sight and all is well with me Words cannot express how good You have been to me. When I ask You to forgive me, You forgive me. When I ask You to help me, You help me. When I ask you to heal me, You heal me. When I ask You to lead me in the way I should go, You lead me. When I ask You to bless my family, You bless them. When I ask You to strengthen me, You do it. When I ask You to deliver me from Satan, the evil one, You do it.

Lord You are good to me. Your mercy endures forever, and I am thankful. With a heart filled with gratitude, I pray and praise You in Jesus' name. Amen.

GOD'S COVENANT

SCRIPTURE REFERENCE

Deuteronomy 7:9

9) *Therefore, know that the Lord your God, He is God, the faithful God who keeps covenant and mercy for a thousand generations with those who love Him and keep His commandments.*

PRAYER

Father, You are God, the only true and living God. You are a merciful God who at my request forgives me for all my sins of commission and omission, through the blood of Jesus. For that I am grateful. Lord, You are a faithful God. You are faithful to keep your covenant with those who love You and keep your commandments.

Thank You for giving me favor and giving favor to my family and even to the generations yet unborn.

Father, I thank You for being my strength when I am weak and for providing those things I have need of, and for healing me when I become sick.

Dear God, I ask that You empower me (your creation, your child) to consistently please You by obeying your commands and exemplifying the character of Jesus.

Father, in times of trouble and times of sorrow, You are my divine source of Joy: Joy unspeakable Joy. Joy that passes all understanding. So, I say thank You.

Lord, because You are an all-powerful God and You love me and I love you, I know all things work together for the good to those who love You and are called according to Your purpose (Romans 8:28). So again, I say thank you.

Father, please fill me with the Holy Spirit, who shall enable me to fulfill the purpose for which I was created.

Almighty God, I love You with all my heart, all my soul, all my mind and strength. In Jesus' name. Amen.

THE HOLY SPIRIT

SCRIPTURE REFERENCE

Ephesians 5:8-10

8)   *For you were once in darkness, but now you are light in the Lord. Walk as children of light.*

9)   *(for the fruit of the Spirit is in all goodness, righteousness and truth),*

10) *finding put what is acceptable to the Lord.*

PRAYER

Lord, I thank You that I am no longer in darkness. Now I walk in the marvelous light of Jesus. I am justified (just as if I never sinned) through my Lord and Savior Christ Jesus. I live in the Spirit. I walk in goodness, righteousness and truth which is the Word of God.

Father, I study the Word of God to ascertain what is acceptable to You. I study Your precepts and obey Your commands in the Holy bible. Lord, You and Your promises are the source of my joy, happiness and peace.

I shall live according to Your will and walk as a child of light; thus, as a child of God in the name of Jesus. Amen.

PROMISE OF GOD

SCRIPTURE REFERENCE

Ephesians 6:2-3

2) *Honor your father and mother, which is the first commandment with promise*

3) *that it may be well with you and you may live long on earth.*

PRAYER

Father God, thank You for giving me life through my mother and daddy. I shall honor them while they are alive and even after death. They may have made some mistakes (everyone has) but I love them and appreciate them. I am who I am because of them and because of the Holy Spirit that lives within me. It is with gratitude, I honor my father and mother.

Lord, I thank You that things have gone well with me. I am deeply grateful for Your kindness, mercy, compassion, favor and for Your promise: based on me honoring my father and mother, I shall have long life on earth. I shall have faith and obey Your commands. Therefore, I shall have long life here on earth and eternal life in Heaven. It is in the name of Jesus I pray. Amen.

GOD IS I AM

SCRIPTURE REFERENCE

Exodus 3:14

14) *And God said to Moses, "I AM WHO I AM". And He said, "Thus, you shall say to the children of Israel, I AM has sent me to you".*

PRAYER

Father, I thank You for being the great and wonderful I AM. Thank You for being the source from whom my needs are met. You are the breath I breathe. You are my strength to walk, my voice to talk and with my voice I shall share the good news. You are my help when I am troubled. You are the Almighty I Am. You are my hope and my joy. You are my refuge, my strong tower and my shield. God, You are my Healer an my Provider of good and perfect gifts. You are the great I AM. You are my Peace that passes all understanding. Father, You are a light unto my path and you are a friend that sticks closer than a brother.

Dear God, You gave Your son, Jesus, to pay the price for my sins that through faith I am saved. Now, my Savior Christ Jesus, is my Mediator, who lives to make intercessions for me. So, I say thank You.

Father I am so grateful that Your Word assures me, You will never leave me nor forsake me, and when the enemy comes in like a flood, You lift up a standard against him. No weapon formed against me shall prosper. You are King of kings and Lord of lords You are the great I AM.

Father, thank You for Your grace and Your mercy. Thank You for being a faithful and loving God. Father, You are Alpha and Omega, the First and the Last, the Beginning and the End, who is and was and is to come. Heavenly Father You give me courage to face tomorrow and the power to fight the good fight of faith. You are the Author and the Finisher of my faith. I worship You because of who You are. You are I AM.

Father God, I thank You, I love You, I honor You and I give You all the glory and all the praise, in the precious name of Jesus. Amen.

GOD HEALS

SCRIPTURE REFERENCE

Exodus 15:26

26) *...diligently heed the voice of the Lord your God and do what is right in His sight, give ear to His commandments...for I am the Lord who heals you.*

PRAYER

Lord God because I hear Your voice and do what is right in Your sight, You are faithful to heal me when I am sick. Thank You for not only healing me each time I am sick, but when events, situations and circumstances break my heart, You heal my broken heart and make me whole. You are the Healer of my body, my mind and my soul.

Almighty God, thank You for Jesus, who by the stripes He took for my sins, I am healed.

Father, I am grateful that You gave Your only begotten son for the sins of humanity. Thus, by faith, one has access to: salvation, peace, prosperity, healing and long life. I worship You and give You all the glory, honor and praise in the name of Jesus. Amen.

THE HOLY SPIRIT

SCRIPTURE REFERENCE

Galatians 5:24-25

24) And those who are Christ's have crucified the flesh with its passions and desires.

25) If we live in the Spirit, let us also walk in the Spirit.

PRAYER

Father, because I study the Word of God, my mind has been renewed, and I have been transformed. Romans 12:2 states "And do not be conformed to this world, but be transformed by the renewing of your mind, that you may prove what is that good and acceptable and perfect will of God". Because I have been transformed, I am no longer controlled by fleshly desires and worldly ways. I live according to the Spirit of God that lives within me. I have put away passions and desire of the flesh. I have put away lying, adultery (sex with someone else's spouse), fornication (sex outside the bond of marriage), slander and the like.

Father, help me to consistently allow the Spirit to control my words, thoughts and actions, not my flesh. I am committed to obeying Your commandments which are enumerated in Deuteronomy 5:16-21 because I love you.

Thank You dear God, for Your mercy, grace, love, forgiveness and provisions in Jesus' name. Amen.

GOD'S PRESENCE

SCRIPTURE REFERENCE

Hebrews 13:5b

5b)   ...be content with such things as you have. For He Himself has said, "I will never leave you nor forsake you".

PRAYER

Father, You said in Your Word that You would never leave me nor forsake me. For that I am grateful.

Dear God, I am depending on Your presence, because I need You every second of my life. I need You when I am at home; I need You when I am working, and I need You when I am at church. I know, I need You always, and You are always with me. Thank You Lord for never leaving me.

Father, You are a great God; You are a loving God; You are a faithful God. You are faithful to keep Your covenant and all Your promises in the Holy bible.

You said that we have not because we ask not. Lord I ask You, in the name of Jesus, save my family and all my loved ones who have not yet committed their lives to You. Father, like You, I desire that none should perish but all should come to repentance.

Lord, I plead the blood of Jesus over the health of my body, soul and Spirit. I pray that the governing bodies of this nation will let Your will be done, not their will, but Your will be done on earth as it is in heaven.

Father, thank You for Your guidance and Your love, as I strive to be more like Jesus. In the precious name of Jesus. Amen.

PRAISE GOD

SCRIPTURE REFERENCE

Hebrews 13:15

15) *Therefore, by Him let us continually offer the sacrifice of praise to God, that is, the fruit of our lips, giving thanks to His name.*

PRAYER

Father, I give You the sacrifice of praise for saving me from the evil one, from sin and condemnation, and for adopting me into the Kingdom of God. I praise You for the Holy Spirit who gives me the power to obey the Word of God. I praise You for being my Fortress against the attacks of the adversary.

I give You the sacrifice of praise for being my strength when I am weak; for being my Peace, even in the midst of trouble; for being my Healer when I am sick and for making me whole. I give You the sacrifice of praise for providing my daily needs.

Father, You are great, Your work is perfect and Your favor is never ending. I praise You for being the source of my joy. I thank you for the name of Jesus, the name which is above every name, and it is in the name of Jesus I pray. Amen.

85

PEACE

SCRIPTURE REFERENCE

Isaiah 26:3

3)   You will keep him in peace, whose mind is stayed on You.

PRAYER

Father, I am aware that You are always with me and in me. Thank You for keeping me in perfect peace. Peace that passes all understanding. You give me peace even when the adversary, Satan, attacks me with affliction and trouble. Father God, I have peace because all things (good/bad) work together for my good because I love You and I am called according to Your purpose.

Dear God, thank You for supernaturally using the bad as well as the good to make a strong laborer for the advancement of the Kingdom of God. Father, as I labor and am empowered by the Holy Spirit, I proclaim Your Kingdom come on earth as it is in heaven.

Dear God, I celebrate the life of Jesus. I celebrate the fact that Jesus paid the price for my sins and I am now saved by faith, and Jesus is my Savior and Lord.

Father, Your Word says: if we declare a thing, it will be established. Therefore, I (Your child) declare love, peace and harmony over my family, my loved ones and all the children of God.

Heavenly Father, as I go about my daily life, I pray that the Holy Spirit will help me to please You in all I say and do. I call on Jesus, because I know there is power in the name of Jesus: power to heal the sick and power to deliver the oppressed.

Thank You Father for perfect peace, if my mind is stayed and focused on You: the great I AM. I pray in the precious name of Jesus. Amen.

REST IN THE LORD GOD

SCRIPTURE REFERENCE

Isaiah 30:15

15) *For thus says the Lord God, the Holy One of Israel: "In returning and rest you shall be saved; in quietness and confidence shall be your strength"*

PRAYER

Father, I do not worry, because I rest in the knowledge that Your will shall be done on earth and in me, as it is in heaven.

Father, let Your perfect will be done in my life. My confidence is in You, because You love me, You take care of me, You lead me in the way I should go, You give me strength to overcome temptation, You enable me to obey the Word of God and to please You in all I say and do. So, I say thank You.

Father, my confidence is possible because I do not depend on my human abilities. Instead, I depend on your supernatural divine abilities.

Lord, regardless of tribulations, You give me strength to press towards the prize of the high calling of God in Christ Jesus. Therefore, I shall complete the purpose for which I was created. Father, I thank You for continuing to bless the people of God. Dear God, I glorify, honor, and praise You in the name of Jesus. Amen.

GOD OUR PROTECTOR

SCRIPTURE REFERENCE

Isaiah 43:2-3

2)   *"When you pass through the waters, I will be with you; and through the rivers, they shall not overflow you. When you walk through the fire, you shall not be burned, nor shall the flame scorch you.*

3)   *For I am the Lord your God, the Holy One of Israel, Your Savior.*

PRAYER

Lord, thank You for being with me, and protecting me each day of my life, regardless to where I am or where I am going. You are my Savior, who not only saved me from darkness and hell, but saved me unto eternal life. Thank You for saving me from known and unknown harm and danger. Thank You, Father, for bringing me through every trial, test tribulation and affliction.

Father, the things which I suffer only draw me closer to You and prepares me for my purpose in life. Weeping may endure for a night, but joy comes in the morning (Psalm 30:5). No (Satanic) weapon formed against me shall prosper (Isaiah 54:17). Therefore, I thank You, Lord for all my experiences, good and bad, which cause me to grow in the things of God.

Lord, You are my God; Jesus is my Savior, and I give You all the glory, honor and praise in the name of Jesus. Amen.

GOD OUR PROTECTOR

SCRIPTURE REFERENCE

Isaiah 59:19b

19b) …When the enemy comes in like a flood, the Spirit of the Lord will lift up a standard against him.

PRAYER

Dear God, thank You for lifting up the standard of Jesus Christ against Satan when he comes in like a flood and he tries to attack me and cause strife in my family. I too rebuke Satan and declare the blood of Jesus is against him. Father, there have been times I would have lost my mind if it had not been for Your favor, protection and love, but just as stated in 2 Timothy 1:7 You have not given me a Spirit of fear, but of power and of love and of a sound mind. So, I say thank You.

Thank You Father for your promise that no weapon formed against me shall prosper. Heavenly Father, for Your Daily benefits, blessings, mercy and favor throughout my life, I shall be eternally grateful. Thank You for the people of God and the angels that surround us.

I praise You Father for the Word of God which delineates Your promises to the children of God and teaches me how to live a life that pleases You. Thank s for Your promise that nothing can separate me from Your awesome love.

Great and Mighty God, I love You for who You are, and I give You all the glory, honor and praise in the name of Jesus. Amen.

THE LORDS GLORY

SCRIPTURE REFERENCE

Isaiah 60:2-3a

2) *For behold, the darkness shall cover the earth and deep darkness the people; but the Lord will arise over you, and His glory will be seen upon you.*

3a) *The Gentiles shall come to light...*

PRAYER

Lord, let the light of Your glory be seen upon me. Father, cause Your light in me and upon me to draw those who do not know You to me, so that I may share the good news and Your great love for them. Father, help me to lead them to accept Jesus as their Lord and Savior. Thus, they will be reconciled with You and will no longer be in darkness, but they will have eternal life.

Father, I praise You for Your Word, for Your glorious light and for Your awesome love, in Jesus name. Amen.

GOD'S WISDOM

James 1:5

5)   *If any of you lacks wisdom, let him ask of God, who gives to all liberally and without reproach, and it will be given to him.*

PRAYER

Dear God, life requires all human beings to make numerous decisions each day, therefore, I ask You to please give me divine wisdom. I want to always please You, and to contribute to the upbuilding of the Kingdom of God.

Father, please help me to maintain those relationships which help and not hinder my divine purpose for which I was created. Help me to discern and avoid those relationships which may be a stumbling block or hindrance to my efforts to live according to the Word of God. Also, Lord, help me to encourage, nurture and cherish the divine relationships which You have ordained to be in my life.

Father God, thank You for placing words of wisdom in my mouth. Lead me where You want me to go. Give me the strength and wisdom to let Your will be done to me, Your will be done in me and Your will be done through me.

Almighty God, help me to lead others to confess their sins, repent and accept Jesus Christ as their Lord and Savior. Empower me to explain to them that the shed blood of Jesus paid the price for their sins so that they may make Jesus their Lord and Savior and have eternal life in heaven and to emphasize the importance of studying and obeying the Word of God (the Bible) and faithfully attending a Bible based church.

Father, I thank You for giving me wisdom in all I do, all I say and in all I think. It is in the precious name of Jesus Christ I pray. Amen.

GOD MY STRENGTH

SCRIPTURE REFERENCE

Joel 3:10b

10b) …Let the weak say 'I am strong.'

PRAYER

Father, thank You for the Word of God. 2 Corinthians 12:9 states: "My grace is sufficient for you, for My strength is made perfect in weakness". Father, when I feel weak, I say I am strong, and Your strength is made perfect in me. Your strength becomes my strength.

Where there is discord in my family or other relationships, I say I am strong. When I feel discouraged, I say I am strong. When I am tired, I say I am strong. When trouble lifts its ugly head, I say I am strong. Lord, You are my strength and I thank You.

Father God, You are omnipotent, all powerful. You are awesome. Thank You for being the source of my strength. You are the source of all that is good and perfect, because You are perfect. I shall continue to seek your face, study Your Word and Your divine way in the name of Jesus. Amen.

GOD MUST INCREASE

SCRIPTURE REFERENCE

John 3:30

30) "He must increase, but I must decrease".

PRAYER

Father God, You are the Great and Mighty God who created the universe. Awesome is Your compassion and Your love. Lord, it is in You I live, move and have my being(Acts17:28). Father, let the spirit of Jesus increase within me. Let there be more of Him and less of me.

Father, help me to live according to the spirit and not according to the lust of the flesh. Place Your desires in my heart and I will follow. I want to be more like Jesus. I want to have the character of Jesus.

Father, fill me fresh and anew with the Holy Spirit, who enables me to obey the Word of God through Christ Jesus. May Your Kingdom come on earth as it is in heaven in Jesus' name. Amen.

EVERLASTING LIFE

SCRIPTURE REFERENCE

John 6:47-48

47) *Most assuredly, I say to you, he who believes in Me has everlasting life.*

48) *"I am the bread of life".*

PRAYER

Dear God, it is because I believe in You and I believe in Jesus, I know I have everlasting life. For that I say thank You. I believe in You, because You first loved me, although I was immersed in sin and unlovable according to the world's standard, You still loved me.

Father I believe in You because every time I became sick, You healed me. I believe in You because when I thought I was going to lose my mind, I cried out to You, and I received peace that passes all understanding. I believe in You because You woke me up this morning. I believe in You, because You sacrificed Your son, Jesus, so that when I believed in Him turned from my sinful worldly ways, I became reconciled with You and I have eternal life. I believe in You, because You are my Provider. You provide all my needs and every good and perfect gift I receive is from You. I believe in You, because You are Alpha and Omega, the First and the Last, the King of kings and the Lord of lords. Lord, I worship You because of who You are.

I love You with all that I am, and all that I hope to become. I thank You, and give You all the glory, all the honor and all the praise. In the magnificent name of Jesus, I pray. Amen.

GOD HEALS

SCRIPTURE REFERENCE

John 11:4

4)   *When Jesus heard that, He said, "This sickness is not unto death, but for the glory of God, that the Son of God may be glorified through it".*

PRAYER

Father, each time I have been sick, You have healed me. My sickness was not unto death, and You used it for the glory of God, that the Son of God may be glorified through it. I shall live and not die that I may fulfill the divine purpose for which You created me. By Jesus' stripes I am healed and made whole to continue the work of the Kingdom of God. Lord, thank You for being my Healer. For Your mercy, grace and love. I give You all the glory, honor and praise.

Father, I shall continue to serve You and the Kingdom of God. I know I have a calling on my life to complete and a legacy to pass on to others. Dear God, it is with unconditional love I pray in Jesus' name. Amen.

KEEP GOD'S COMMANDMENTS

SCRIPTURE REFERENCE

John 14:20b, 21

20b) ...I am in My Father, and you in Me, and I in you.

21) He who has My commandments and keeps them, it is he who loves Me, and he who loves Me will be loved by My Father, and I will love him (mankind) and manifest Myself to him.

PRAYER

Lord, thank You for being in me, because I have asked You to be my Lord and Savior. My heart is filled with love for You and all mankind (male and female) regardless to their race, belief or status in life. We are all created by God who loves us.

Father God Because I love You, I keep Your commandments. Thank You, Lord God for Your unconditional love. Thank You for manifesting: Your presence, Your will and Your way to me. I am continually aware that You are with me to: abundantly bless me, guide me, protect me, heal me and deliver me from the oppression of the evil one.

Father God, You are my Hope and my Source of every good and perfect gift. You are the Source of everything I need. So, I say thank You.

Heavenly Father, I praise You and worship You because of who You are. I give You all the glory and honor in the name of Jesus. Amen.

KEEP GOD'S COMMANDMENTS

SCRIPTURE REFERENCE

1 John 3:22

22) *And whatsoever we ask we receive from Him, because we keep His commandments and do those things that are pleasing in His sight.*

PRAYER

Father, I know it is pleasing to You when I keep Your commandments and my life reflects the character of Jesus. I thank You for the Holy Spirit who empowers me to obey the Word of God. As a result, I have faith that what I ask in prayer, I shall receive. So, I say thank You.

Dear God, I proclaim, declare and decree Satan's attempt to kill, steal and destroy my purpose and destiny is null and void in Jesus name. The enemy, Satan, is a defeated foe.

Father, thank You for helping me to walk in divine strength, divine power and divine commitment to reach the lost, and to bring them to the saving knowledge of the Lord. I pray that they, the same as I, shall have the mind and the heart to seek an intimate relationship with God the Father, God the Son and God the Holy Spirit.

Lord, I proclaim victory in their lives, as well as mine, as we live, move and have our being in Christ Jesus.

Heavenly Father, I love You and thank You for loving me. I pray in thee awesome and precious name of Jesus. Amen.

THE HOLY SPIRIT

SCRIPTURE REFERENCE

John 14:26

26) *But the Helper, the Holy Spirit, whom the Father will send in My name, He will teach you all things, and bring to your remembrance all things that I said to you.*

PRAYER

Lord, I thank You Holy Spirit, who helps me, comfort me and who brings to my memory scriptures which delineates your promises, precepts and commands. I shall continue to show myself approved by studying the Holy Bible and applying its truth to my life.

Father, the Holy Spirit, my Helper and my Comforter brings me peace in the midst of trials, tribulations and tests. For His help, I say thank You.

Heavenly Father, I shall "continually offer the sacrifice of praise to (You), that is, the fruit of (my) lips, giving thanks to (Your) name". (Hebrews 13:15). Father, once again, thank You for the Holy Spirit in the name of Jesus. Amen.

Friends of God

Scripture Reference

John 15:14

14) "You are My friends, if you do whatever I command you".
Thank You Lord, for calling me Your friend, because I do whatever You command me to do.

Prayer

Thank You Lord, for calling me Your friend, because I do whatever You command me to do. Father, it is awesome to be called a friend of God. I acknowledge You are the Creator of heaven, earth and all that exists. Father, my finite mind can hardly conceive of the Creator of the Universe calling me friend and loving me so much. However, I know You are not a man that You should lie. So, I say thank You.

Father, you are a good God; You are a great God, You are a powerful God, You are the King of kings and the Lord of lords, yet You call me friend.

Lord, You are the great I AM", my Provider; You are my Strong Tower and my Refuge in the time of trouble. You are the Author and Finisher of my faith and You call me friend.

Thank You for being whatever I need, whenever I need it. You are my all and all. Father, I thank You for my family and my godly relationships. Dear God, fill me with the Holy Spirit who teaches me and enables me to live according to Your Word.

Father, thank You for Your mercy, Your unmerited favor upon my life and for calling me Your friend.

I love You Lord, I love You and again I say I love You. It is in the name which is above every name, the name of Jesus that I pray. Amen.

LOVE

SCRIPTURE REFERENCE

1 John 4:7-8

7)   *Beloved, let us love one another, for love is of God; and everyone who loves is born of God and knows God.*

8)   *He who does not love does not know God, for God is Love.*

PRAYER

Father, I come today to express my love for You, and my love for all human beings. Lord, I thank You for Your Spirit which lives in me. It is because You are Love and You live in me, I am able to love others with the love of God.

I love You Lord and I thank You for loving me even when I was a sinner. I thank You for redeeming me and for bringing me into Your marvelous light. Thank You for adopting me into Your family, the family of God.

Lord, You are: my Creator, my Savior, my Provider, my Healer and my Righteousness. You are my source of peace, and my ever-present Help. You never leave me nor forsake me; so, I say thank You.

Dear God, help me to replace my self-centered desires and will, with Your desires and will. Not my will be done, but Your will be done to me, in me and through me. Let Your will be done on earth as it is in heaven.

Lord, enable me to exemplify the character of Jesus, in my behavior, my deeds, my walk and my talk.

I love You Father, with all my heart, with all my mind with all my soul and with all my strength and I love my neighbor as myself. It is in the awesome name of Jesus I pray. Amen.

LOVE OF GOD

SCRIPTURE REFERENCE

1 John 4:8

8)   *He who does not love does not know God, for God is Love.*

PRAYER

Father God, thank You for Your great love for me, for You are Love. It is because Your love is so great, that You gave Your only begotten Son, Jesus, to die and pay the price for my sins and the sin of others who repented and made Jesus their Lord and Savior. We have been called out of darkness into Your marvelous light, and we have eternal life. Thank You Father, for Jesus and Your great love.

Lord, I love my parents, but Your love is greater: I love my family, but Your love is greater. I love my significant other and my friends, but Your love is greater, because You are Love. So, I say thank You.

Almighty God, when I am sick, I say by Jesus' stripes, I am healed and what I decree is done. God, You open the windows of heaven and pour out blessings upon me and my family. And just as you said, You supply all our needs according to Your riches in glory. Father, for every good gift and every perfect gift You give me, I say thank You.

Father, Your love abides in my heart. Therefore, I love every human being regardless of race, color, creed or status in life. All this is true because You are Love and You live within me.

Dear God, the Father, God the Son and God the Holy Spirit, my prayer, praise, prose and poem to You are to say:
When I think of love, I think of You because You are Love.
Regardless too trouble, disappointment, pain and sorrow,
I look with expectation to god, Jesus and tomorrow.
I hold my head up high,
Not in false pride, but to reach the sky.
I know Jesus looks at me from there:
with great love and deep care.
Lord, I just want to say:
My desire is to give You honor and to obey;
Forever, in every way.
Father, without being haughty, I lift my head toward You above,
And I rejoice in Your unconditional, awesome Love!
It is in the precious name of Jesus I give You honor, I praise You and I pray. Amen.

VICTORY

SCRIPTURE REFERENCE

John 5:4

4)   *For whatever is born of God overcomes the world. And this is the victory that has overcome the world- our faith.*

PRAYER

Father, thank You that by faith I have accepted Jesus as my Savior and I have overcome the world. I have victory over the deceitful tricks of the devil.

Almighty God, thank You for loving me and being my help in times of troubles. No matter what I go through, Father, I know no weapon formed against me shall prosper, because You are with me. You are an awesome God. Greater are You in me than he who is in the world.

Lord, I am at peace because You are my peace. You said: all things work together for good, if I love You and I am called according to Your purpose.

Dear God, I know that my light afflictions are merely part of the process which leads to the manifestation of my divine destination. I know that every good gift and every perfect gift is from You, the Father of lights; so, I say thank You.

Heavenly Father, I ask You to heal me when I need to be healed, whether physically, emotionally, mentally or spiritually. Thank You for blessing my family, my relationships, my finances and my efforts to serve and live according to Your divine will.

Father, I am committed to obeying the inspired Word of God (the Holy Bible), which is the instruction manual for living a righteous life. Thank You for a victorious life in the name of Jesus. Amen.

GOD OUR PROTECTOR

SCRIPTURE REFERENCE

Isaiah 43: 2-3

2)   *"When you pass through the waters, I will be with you; and through the rivers, they shall not overflow you. When you walk through the fire, you shall not be burned, nor shall the flame scorch you.*

3)   *For I am the Lord your God, the Holy One of Israel, your Savior.*

PRAYER

Lord, thank You for being with me, and protecting me each day of my life, regardless to where I am or where I am going. You are my Savior, who not only saved me from darkness and hell, but saved me unto eternal life. Thank You Father for bringing me through every trial, test, tribulation and affliction.

Father, the things which I suffer only draw me closer to You and prepares me for my purpose in life. Weeping may endure for a night, but joy comes in the morning (Psalm 30:5). No (Satanic) weapon formed against me shall prosper (Isaiah 54:17). Therefore, I thank You Lord for all my experiences, good or bad, which cause me to grow in the things of God.

Lord, You are my God; Jesus is my Savior and I give You all the glory, honor and praise in the name of Jesus. Amen.

GOD'S MERCY AND COMPASSION

SCRIPTURE REFERENCE

Lamentations 3:22-23

22) *Through the Lord's mercies we are not consumed, because His compassions fail not*

23) *They are new every morning; great is Your faithfulness.*

PRAYER

Lord, I know You are faithful and compassionate therefore, my hope is in You. It is because of Your compassion and mercy, when I am discouraged, You are my courage, when I am sad, You are my comforter, when I am depressed, I am confident that I have a blessed and bright future.

Father, because Your mercy is new every morning: You are my sufficiency. You are my all and all. You are my everything. Father, I am grateful that Your mercy, faithfulness and compassion are new every morning. So, I say thank You. Thank You for Your eternal love. I praise You because of who You are, and because it is in You I have hope, peace, and Joy by the power of the Holy Spirit. I look to Jesus, who is the author and finisher of my faith. Dear God, I ask that You bless and refresh Your children, the people of God in the name of Jesus. Amen.

JESUS OUR SAVIOR

Luke 2:11

11)   *For there is born to you this day in the city of David a Savior, who is Christ the Lord.*

PRAYER

Father, I celebrate Jesus, who is my Savior. Lord when I experience sadness, pain, disappointment or loneliness, I replace those feelings with thoughts of Jesus who is the center of my Joy.

Father, I am grateful for the birth, life, death and resurrection of Jesus the Christ, who enabled me to receive salvation by faith. I thank You Father, for Jesus who sent us the Comforter: The Holy Spirit. I cannot make it on my own. It is by the power of the Holy Spirit, I am able to resist and overcome temptation, and obey the will of God as recorded in the Holy Bible.

Father, You are the giver of every good gift and every perfect gift to me and the people of God. Thank You for the greatest gift of all: the gift of Jesus Christ.

Father, I confess that I sometimes miss the mark and make poor choices which result in bad experiences. Nevertheless, I repent, and I believes as Romans 8:28 states: "And we know that all things work together for good to those who love God, to those who are the called according to (God's) purpose". For this I say thank You.

Dear God, I reiterate the praise of the angels and the heavenly host, when Jesus was born more than 2000 years ago, I say, "Glory to God in the highest, and on earth, peace and goodwill toward men". Lord, I revere You, I love You, I adore You, I honor You, I worship You and give You all the glory and praise. In the precious name of Jesus, I pray. Amen.

POWER IN THE NAME OF JESUS

SCRIPTURE REFERENCE

Luke 9:1

1) *Then He called His twelve disciples together and gave them power and authority over all demons and to cure diseases".*

PRAYER

Dear God, thank You for giving me power and authority over all demons in the name of Jesus. By faith I come against demonic spirits that attack my life in Jesus name. I declared and decree it is done in that name which is above every name, the name of Jesus.

In the name of Jesus, I rebuke You Satan and demand that the demonic attacks of oppression and depression against me cease and desist.

Father, because greater is He that is in me than he that is in the world and as stated in 1 Corinthians 15:57 You give me the victory through our Lord Jesus Christ, I say thank You.

Thank You, Lord Jesus, for interceding on my behalf; thank You for praying that I prosper and abound in my health, in my godly desires, in my relationships, in my peace of mind, in my growth in the things of God and in my Joy in the Lord.

Father, I request that You place the desire to study the Word of God daily in my heart, that I may show myself approved. I blessed Your Holy name. It is in the name of Jesus I pray. Amen.

YOU SHALL HAVE WHAT YOU SAY

SCRIPTURE REFERENCE

Mark 11:23

23) *"For assuredly, I say to you, whoever says to this mountain, 'Be removed and be cast into the sea', and does not doubt in his heart, but believes that those things he says will be done, he will have whatever he says".*

PRAYER

Lord, today I believe and have no doubt, I shall have what I say. Father, it is with faith that I declare I will have a breakthrough. I declare the angels who have been dispatched on my behalf, will breakthrough and bring forth abundant blessings according to Your will.

Heavenly Father, I thank You for the manifestation of Your divine favor in my life. Thank you for uniting my household in greater love and unity. Thank You for new God ordained relationships that shall last a lifetime. Thank You for healing my body and soul. Dear God, increase my knowledge, understanding and wisdom as I study the Word of God, the Bible.

Thank You for Your mercy, financial blessings and love. Father, there is power in the name of Jesus. Through my faith in Jesus Christ who paid the price for my sins, I am saved. Lord, I don't have the words to express my gratitude.

Father, Your Word says faith without works is dead. I ask You to increase my strength and zeal to accomplish the divine deeds and godly desires You have placed in my heart. It is my deep desire to be used by You according to Your will.

Father, I do believe those things I pray, and those things I say, will come to pass, in Jesus name. Amen.

SAVIOR

SCRIPTURE REFERENCE

Matthew 1:21

21) *And she will bring forth a Son, and you shall call His name Jesus, for He will save His people from their sins.*

PRAYER

Father, I thank You for Jesus, who paid the price for my sins. I thank You for enabling me by Your Spirit to obey Your Word and to exemplify the character of Jesus Christ. I know You will answer my prayers based on Your infinite knowledge of what is best for me. So, I say thank You.

Dear God, I stand against Satan's efforts to steal, kill and destroy my purpose and destiny. I proclaim, declare and decree: his attempts are null and void. The enemy is a defeated foe. Thank You Father, for giving me victory, as I live, move and have my being according to Your good, acceptable and perfect will.

Father, help me to continue to reach the lost and teach the found. Lord, I pray that they shall be saved and have the heart and mind to seek an intimate relationship with God the Father and God the Son. Father, I love You and I thank You for loving me. I pray in the awesome and precious name of Jesus. Amen.

WORDS OF GOD

SCRIPTURE REFERENCE

Matthew 4:4

4)   *But He answered and said, "It is written, man shall not live by bread alone, but by every word that proceeds from the mouth of God".*

PRAYER

Father God, help me to live by every word that proceeds from Your mouth. I thank You for the Word of God, the Holy Bible, which states in Acts 17:28: it is in You "we live, move and have our being". Your Word also tells me that You "give to all life, breath and all thigs". Acts 17:25

Father, I thank You for life and all the things You have given me. You fill my life with Your favor, Your mercy, Your protection and Your abundant blessings.

Thank You Dear God, for giving me the desire, the strength and the boldness to witness to others and tell them about Your deeds and wondrous works. Help me to be as bold as a lion when I tell of Your goodness, Your unconditional love and assure them that You will never leave them nor forsake them. Father, You are my peace that passes all understanding. You are my Provider of every good and perfect gift, You are my everything. So, I say thank You.

Dear God, You are so awesome, so amazing and so wonderful. I am grateful that You call me Your child, Your beloved and the apple of Your eye. I am committed to obeying You, to pleasing You and letting Your will be done to me, in me and through me. Father, I am dedicated to living by every word that proceeds from Your mouth in Jesus name. Amen.

133

Obey the Will of God

Scripture Reference

Matthew 7:21

21)   *"Not everyone who says to Me, Lord, Lord, shall enter the kingdom
of heaven, but he who does the will of my Father in heaven".*

Prayer

Heavenly Father, my deepest desire is to let Your will be done
in me and through me. Not my will, but Your will, because Your
will is perfect. Because of my faith, Jesus lives within me. By faith
in Jesus Christ, I have been justified, just as if I never sinned
(Galatians2:16). I have become the righteousness of God through
Jesus (2 Corinthians 5:21).

Father, thank You for filling me with the Holy Spirit, who gives
me the power (Acts 1:8) to be a witness and to obey Your will, Your
Word and Your Way.

Lord, thank You for adopting me into the family of God as heir
and joint heir with Christ (Romans 8:16-17). Praise You Lord. It
is because of Your grace, (Your favor), I shall enter the kingdom of
heaven and I shall have eternal life. Lord, I give You all the glory,
honor and praise in the name of Jesus. Amen.

LOVE

SCRIPTURE REFERENCE

Matthew 22:37-39

37)   *Jesus said to him, "You shall love the Lord your God with all your heart, with all your soul, and with all your mind.*

38)   *This is the first and great commandment.*

39)   *And the second is like it. 'You shall love your neighbor as yourself.'*

PRAYER

Father, I love You with all my heart, all my soul and all my mind. I know You loved me even before I knew You. There is no greater love than Your love, because You gave Your only son, to die and pay the price for my sins so that by faith I could be saved. For that, I am deeply grateful. Thank You for loving me unconditionally.

Father, I love myself because You created me in Your image (Genesis 1:27) and I am fearfully and wonderfully made (Psalm 139:14). Dear God, I love all people because You live in me and You are love. I let Your love and light radiate from me through my smile, through my caring, compassion and deeds. Lord God, I give You all the glory, honor and praise in Jesus' name. Amen.

PEOPLE OF GOD

SCRIPTURE REFERENCE

1 Peter 2:9, 10a

9)   *But you are a chosen generation, a royal priesthood, a holy nation,
     His own special people that you may proclaim the praises of Him
     who called you out of darkness into His marvelous light;*

10a) *who once were not a people but are now the people of God.*

PRAYER

Father, thank You for calling me out of Satan's world of darkness
into Your marvelous, heavenly light, and for declaring that I am
now a part of the people of God. Because I have faith. I am one of
the heirs of God and joint heirs with Christ. (Romans 8: 17).

I praise You Lord, with my whole heart and shall continually
tell of Your goodness. I am not ashamed of the gospel of Christ,
for it is the power of God to salvation for everyone who believes...
(Romans 1:16). Father, I shall continue to obey the Word of God,
(the Holy Bible) and tell of Your good works. I totally surrender my
will to You, to Your will, to Your Word, and to Your way. I shall share
the good news of the gospel and the testimony of Your goodness. In
Jesus name, Amen.

GRACE AND PEACE

Peter 1:2

2)   *Grace and peace be multiplied to you in the knowledge of God and of Jesus our Lord.*

PRAYER

Lord, I thank You for Your grace and peace. Father, it is because of Your grace, (the gift of undeserved favor) that I have life. Father, I know that Jesus came to the world that we may be saved and have life and that more abundantly. For that I say thank You.

Father, it is by Your grace and Your mercy that I have the peace of God that passes all understanding. I have peace regardless to my circumstances, regardless to what is going on in my finances, my health, my home, my family, the world, or in my relationships. Father, the joy of the Lord is my strength. So, Father, I thank You for Your mercy, Your grace and peace that passes all understanding.

Father, most of all, I thank You for Jesus. It is because of Jesus and Your grace that I am able to receive salvation. It is by my faith and belief in the death, burial and resurrection of Jesus, the son of God who paid the price for my sins with His own blood that I am saved and adopted into the family of God. For Your saving grace. I say thank You.

Dear God, it is in the name of Jesus that I thank You for multiplying grace, blessings and peace in my life that I pray. Amen.

A Good Work in You

Scripture Reference

Philippians 1:6

6) .... He who has begun a good work in you will complete it until the day of Jesus Christ.

Prayer

Father continue to do a good work in me. Please continue to: renew my mind with Your Word, to give me peace that passes all understanding and to fill me with the Holy Spirit. Father, I totally give myself to You, so that You may use me to do the work of the Kingdom of God. God, transform me into Your image with the character of Jesus Christ.

I declare and decree that the good work You have begun in me shall be completed. I shall complete the purpose for which I was created. I shall complete the divine work You want me to do. I will fulfill my destiny, so when I come to heaven, You will say "well done, good and faithful servant" (Matthew 25:21) It is in the name of Jesus. I pray amen.

External Life

Scripture Reference

Philippians 1:21

21) For to me, to live is Christ, and to die is gain.

Prayer

Father, I live to fulfill the divine desires You place in my heart through Christ within me. Thank You for the good work the Holy Spirit enables me to do. As I work as unto the Lord, I shall share the good news of the Gospel and declare your many good works. May my good works glorify You. Be glorified, Father, as I tithe 10% of my increase, give to the poor, exemplify love to all mankind and pray for others. Thank You for Your unconditional love.

Father, as long as I live, please use my hands, my feet, my voice, and my deeds as conduit to bring about Your Kingdom here on earth as it is in heaven.

Lord, thank You so much for long life. Nevertheless, I am not afraid of death, because to die is gain. I shall gain eternal life with You in Heaven. Father, while I live on earth, I shall give You all the glory, honor and praise. In Jesus' name, Amen.

JESUS THE NAME
ABOVE EVERY NAME

SCRIPTURE REFERENCE

Philippians 2:9-11

9) *Therefore, God also has highly exalted Him and given Him the name which is above every name,*

10) *that at the name of Jesus, every knee should bow, of those in heaven, and of those on earth and of those under the earth,*

11) *and every tongue should confess that Jesus Christ is Lord, to the glory of God the Father.*

PRAYER

Father, I exalt the name of Jesus today; it is the name that is above every name. I acknowledge and declare Jesus is Lord. I invite Jesus to be the Lord over my life, over my relationships, my family, my finances, and my destiny. Father, I surrender to Your will and not my will. I ask that Your will be done in me, to me and through me.

Satan, the blood of Jesus is against you. I rebuke you and bind your efforts to kill my faith, steal my joy and destroy my destiny.

Holy Spirit empower me to please the Lord in all I do, say and think. You are worthy, O' Lord, to receive glory, honor and praise. Father, You are all powerful, You created all things, and the Bible tells us that mankind was created for Your pleasure.

Dear God, I thank You for the favor You have given the people of God. I thank You for all You do and for who You are. I pray in the name that is above every name: the name of Jesus. Amen.

Reach Forward to the Future

Scripture Reference

Philippians 3:13

13)   Brethren… one thing I do, forgetting those things which are behind and reaching forward to those things which are ahead.

Prayer

Father, I know my past prepared me for my present and future, but I am careful to think of those things which are ahead instead of the past. I look forward because 3rd John 2 states "I may prosper in all things and be in health, just as (my) soul prospers". Father, I thank You that there are things you have prepared for me before the foundation of the world. I shall follow where Your Spirit leads me and I shall obey the Word of God. I shall "press toward the goal for the prize of the upward call of God in Christ Jesus" Philippians 3:14.

Dear God, use me as Your conduit through which Your plans, desires and will be done on earth as it is in heaven through Jesus Christ.

Thank You Father for Your mercy and grace in the name of Jesus. Amen

149

Purpose and Destiny

Scripture Reference

Philippians 3:14

14) I press toward the goal for the prize of the upward call of God in Christ Jesus.

Prayer

Father, I press toward the goal for the prize of the upward call of God, and finally You will give me "the crown of righteousness" (2 Timothy 4:8).

Lord, I press towards my destiny and my purpose in life which You reveal to me month by month, week by week and day by day.

Father, help me not to miss the mark of Your high calling. I depend on Your divine assistance to enable me to "walk worthy of the calling with which (I was) called (Ephesians 4:1). Dear God, I give You all the glory, honor and praise in the precious name of Jesus. Amen.

REJOICE IN THE LORD

SCRIPTURE REFERENCE

Philippians 4:4

4)   Rejoice in the Lord always. Again, I will say rejoice!

PRAYER

Dear God, I rejoice today because I have hope. My hope is in You, regardless to the stress that might be in my life. I rejoice because the angels encamped around me as a hedge of protection against evil, and I am safe. Father, I rejoice because You hear my prayers and You will answer.

Father, it is not about me, but it is all about You and who You are. You are omnipotent. You are an all-powerful God. You are omniscient. You are an all-knowing God. You know my past, my present and my future. You prosper me and not harm me. You give me hope and a future. Lord, I rejoice in You and say thank You.

Lord, I rejoice in who You are. Words cannot express how grateful I am and how much I love You. So, I just say, I love You Lord. I rejoice in You and again I say, I rejoice in You! It is in the precious name of Jesus I pray. Amen.

MEDITATE

SCRIPTURE REFERENCE

Philippians 4:8

8)   *Finally, brethren, whatever things are true, whatever things are noble, whatever things are just, whatever things are pure, whatever things are lovely, whatever things are of good report, if there is any virtue and if there is anything praiseworthy - meditate on these things.*

PRAYER

Father, thank You for delivering me from stress. I shall not be anxious about anything, because You are my shepherd and I shall not want. You Father are my Provider of everything I need.

Father, thank You for the Holy Spirit who reminds me to meditate on those things which are true, noble, just, pure, lovely, good, and praiseworthy.

Satan, I rebuke you and your efforts to put negative thoughts in my mind. The blood of Jesus is against you.

Father God, I shall meditate on Jesus my Savior and on the Word of God, which is my guide on how to live each day. Thank You Father God, for answering my prayers in the name of Jesus, the Christ. Amen.

GOD IS MY STRENGTH

SCRIPTURE REFERENCE

Philippians 4:13

13)   I can do all things through Christ who strengthens me.

PRAYER

Father, I come to You with thanksgiving. I thank You for strengthening me to not only be a hearer of the Word of God, but a doer of Your will.

When I feel weak, I am reminded that Your strength is made perfect in weakness. (2 Corinthians 12:9). My weakness is replaced by Your strength.

Heavenly Father, it is because of Your favor, Your might, Your strength and Your spirit within me. I am empowered through Christ to do all things which are aligned with the scriptures in the Word of God. When I speak a promise that is written in the Holy Bible, it will come to pass. It shall be manifested.

Father, I pray that You lead me in the path of righteousness each day that I may please You and all I say, think and do. I praise Your Holy name in the awesome name of Jesus. Amen

TRUST IN THE LORD

SCRIPTURE REFERENCE

Proverbs 3:5-6

5) *Trust in the Lord with all your heart and lean not on your own understanding;*

6) *In all your ways acknowledge Him and He shall direct your paths.*

PRAYER

Lord, I acknowledge You are great, You are good, You are gentle, You are gracious, You are kind and You are faithful. Thank You for giving me unmerited favor.

Father, my trust is in You. My trust is in the Word of God, and my trust is in Your love and faithfulness. I know that I am alive today because of Your mercy and love. I am aware that You are always with me and You will never leave me nor forsake me.

Thank You for creating me for Your divine purpose. Father illuminate and manifest that purpose in my heart, spirit, and soul. Lord, I acknowledge that I depend on You and ask You to direct me in the path of righteousness: the path which pleases and glorifies You.

I love You Lord, and thank You for Your ever present, everlasting love for me and all mankind. I pray in that name which is above every name, the name of Jesus. Amen.

159

CONFIDENCE

SCRIPTURE REFERENCE

Proverbs 3:26, 33b-34b

26)   For the Lord will be your confidence...
33b) ...He blesses the home of the just.
34b) gives grace to the humble.

PRAYER

Lord, my confidence is not in my human abilities: my confidence is in You, in Your love, in Your kindness, in Your mercy, in Your grace and in Your guidance. Father, because of my faith and what Christ did, You call me justified, You call me righteous. As a result, You bless my home and my family. I am grateful for these blessing and all other blessings.

Thank You for grace (unmerited favor) You give me each day. I commit my entire life to You, Your will, and Your authority. You are my Lord and Savior. Thank you for divine confidence, justification and grace.

Father, I give You glory, honor and praise, for You are Lord of lords and King of kings. You are the great I Am. With a humble heart, I thank You Father God, for Your mercy, Your love and Your grace in the name of Jesus. Amen.

The Lord is a Strong Tower

Scripture Reference

Proverbs 18:10

10) *The name of the Lord is a strong tower, the righteous run to it and are safe.*

Prayer

Lord, I was created to give You glory and honor. You are worthy to receive my heart felt praise because of who You are. You are my strong tower. I run to You and I am safe. You are the Alpha and the Omega, the First and the Last, the Beginning and the End. You are the sovereign and eternal God. You are everything to me. For who You are, I praise you.

Lord, You Are Jehovah Jireh my Provider. Just as You provided Abraham a ram in the thicket, You provide me shelter, the food that I eat, the clothes I wear, and the air I breathe. For who You, I praise You,

Lord, You are Jehovah Rapha, my Healer. Thank You for healing my body, my mind, and my emotions. For who You are, I praise You. Father, You are Jehovah Nissi, my Banner. Because of who You are in my life I have victory over the enemy, the devil. For who You are, I praise you Lord, You are Jehovah Rohi, my shepherd. You take care of me, You watch over me, protect me and feed me with the Word of God. Father, I praise You for being my strong tower, to whom I run, and I am safe. In the precious name of Jesus I pray. Amen.

163

PEACE AND SAFETY

SCRIPTURE REFERENCE

Psalm 4:8

8)   *I will both lie down in peace and sleep; for You alone, O Lord, make me dwell in safety.*

PRAYER

Lord, You are the source of my safety. You protect me: night and day, spring and summer, fall and winter. I am safe at home and away from home. You keep me safe when I travel by automobile, bus, train, and plane. I am safe in the city and safe in the country. Thank You Father, for giving me peace so that I am able to sleep at night soundly and safely.

Lord, you are the Prince of Peace. Thank You Lord for: peace in my home, peace within my family, peace of mind and for being the source of my safety. I give you all the glory, honor and praise in the precious name of Jesus. Amen.

TRUST IN THE LORD

SCRIPTURE REFERENCE

Psalm 5:11, 12

11) *But let all those rejoice who put their trust in You; Let them ever shout for joy, because You defend them; Let those also who love Your name, be joyful in You.*

12) *For You, O Lord, will bless the righteous; with favor. You will surround him as with a shield.*

PRAYER

Lord, in my heart I rejoiced because I trust You. Thinking of You brings me joy, because I love You and I know You love me. I love who You are. I love the name of Jesus. It is in the name of Jesus I am saved; in the name of Jesus, I am healed and protected from harm and danger.

Father, I trust You to lead me in the path of righteousness. It is when I follow You, I am in right standing with You.

Dear God, I rejoice because You bless me and give me favor each day of my life. Thank You for surrounding me as a shield and protecting me whereby the adversary, Satan, is defeated.

Father, You are great and greatly to be praised. You are merciful and faithful. It is with a heart of thanksgiving, I pray in the precious name of Jesus. Amen.

GOD'S WAY IS PERFECT

SCRIPTURE REFERENCE

Psalm 18:30-32

30) As for God, His way is perfect; the word of the Lord is proven; He is a shield to all who trust in Him.

31) For who is God, except the Lord? And who is a rock except our God?

33) It is God who arms me with strength, and makes my way perfect.

PRAYER

Father God, Your way is perfect, flawless, impeccable. Thank You Father for Your shield of protection that surrounds me because I trust You. I trust You God and You are my Rock. You fortify me with strength to live according to Your Word, and Your will, and You make my way perfect.

Lord, I shall pray and obey. I shall obey Your Word which is proven and true. Please endow me with the character of my Savior, Jesus, that I may please You each day in all I say and do. Thank You God, for making my way perfect, in the name of Jesus Christ. Amen.

FEAR NO EVIL

SCRIPTURE REFERENCE

Psalm 23: 3, 4, 6

3) *He restores my soul; He leads me in paths of righteousness for His name's sake.*

4) *... I will fear no evil, for You are with me, Your rod and Your staff, they comfort me.*

6) *Surely goodness and mercy shall follow me all the days of my life; and I will dwell in the house of the Lord forever.*

PRAYER

Dear God, thank You for the Holy Bible: my instruction manual for living according to Your will.

Father, although there is so much evil in the world, I asked You to protect me, therefore, I fear no evil for You are with me, in me, and around me.

Lord, You lead me in the path of righteousness. Thank You for decreeing that I am in right standing with You and that I shall dwell in the house of the Lord forever. I praise You Omnipotent, Omniscient, Omnipresent God in the name of Your Son Jesus. Amen.

WAIT ON THE LORD

SCRIPTURE REFERENCE

Psalm 27:14

14) *Wait on the Lord; be of good courage, and He shall strengthen your heart; wait, I say, on the Lord!*

PRAYER

Father, I love You and praise You. I shall stand on Your Word and wait on the Lord. As I wait Father, I am encouraged because I know "Eye has not seen, nor ear heard, nor have entered into the heart of man the things which God has prepared for those who love Him. (1 Corinthians 2:9)

Father, I shall wait for Your will to be done in my life, and I am not discouraged, because I know the best is yet to come.

Lord, let Your character and Your love shine in me, on me and through me. Help me to boldly lift up the name of Jesus and draw others unto Your saving grace.

Dear God, I know Your will is perfect and You are always on time, therefore, I shall continue to prayerfully and patiently wait on the Lord: my Strength and my Redeemer. It is in the name of Jesus I pray. Amen.

FAVOR OF GOD

SCRIPTURE REFERENCE

Psalm 30:5b

5b)   .... His favor is for life; weeping may endure for a night, but joy comes in the morning.

PRAYER

Thank You, Father, for the unmerited favor You give me each day in every way. I may weep over the death of a family member or another loved one, but I know weeping may endure for a night, but joy comes in the morning; Joy comes in due season.

Father, although Satan tries to oppress me and cause me to be depressed, You deliver me and strengthen me to overcome the attacks of the evil one. I shall share and record in a journal my testimonies of Your goodness, favor and abundant blessings.

Thanks to You God, my Father, my Daddy, for Your awesome favor and for being my strength when I am weak. I may weep for a night, but joy comes in the morning. You are my shepherd and my eternal joy. I give You all the glory, honor and praise. In Jesus' name. Amen.

175

DELIGHT YOURSELF IN THE LORD

SCRIPTURE REFERENCE

Psalm 37:4

4)   *Delight yourself also in the Lord, and He shall give you the desires of your heart.*

PRAYER

Lord, I thank You that it is because I delight myself in knowing You and obeying You, You give me the desires of my heart. I thank You for all the good gifts and the perfect gifts You provide. Thank you that it is because of You that I live, move, and have my being.

Thank You for giving me the divine desire to: 1) please You and to serve You with excellence, 2) to exemplify the character and the nature of Jesus to my family, my loved ones, my friends, my neighbors and all those I meet.

Dear God, I know true leaders are servants. Thank You for giving me a spirit of servant hood and for giving me the desire to serve others.

Father, I asked You to use me according to Your will. I commit myself to Your will, not my will be done, but Your will be done to me in me and through me. Thank You for giving me a blessed and abundant life. Dear God, I love You. You are my Father, my Lord and my King, now and throughout eternity. I thank You for the perfect gift, whose name is Jesus. It is in the precious name of Jesus. I pray. Amen.

Put a Smile on Your Face

Scripture Reference

Psalm 42:5 Message Bible

5) *"Why are you down in the dumps, dear soul? Why are you crying the blues? Fix my eyes on God- soon I'll be praising again. He puts a smile on my face. He's my God".*

Prayer

Father, I smile as I fix my eyes on You. You are the source of my joy and the joy of the Lord is my strength. Father, it is the smile You put on my face that encourages, edifies and imparts love to others. So I say thank you.

Savior, King of kings and Lord of lords, You are worthy of the highest praise. I say, hallelujah. Hallelujah, for You are the great I AM.

Dear God, You are awesome. I worship You for who You are. You are the Creator of mankind and the entire Universe. You are my Healer. My Peace that passes all understanding. You are my Hope and my Refuge when there is trouble. You are my Provider and the giver of every good and perfect gift. When my heart is broken, You are my Comforter. So I say thank You.

Dear God, thank You for Jesus who paid the price for my sins with his own blood. Now, it is my faith in You and Jesus that I am saved; I have the Spirit of Jesus within me. Lord, when I attend church and hear the Word of God preached, I shall not only hear the Word, but I shall be a doer of the Word. Each day I shall obey the Word of God. Father, thank You for Your unconditional love and for promising me that You will never leave me nor forsake me. I love You and give You all the glory, honor and praise in the name of Jesus. Amen.

VOICE OF TRIUMPH

SCRIPTURE REFERENCE

Psalm 47:1, 2

1) *Oh, clap your hands all you peoples! Shout to God with a voice of triumph!*
2) *For the Lord Most High is awesome; He is a great King over all the earth.*

PRAYER

Father and Most High Lord, You are awesome. You are King of kings and Lord of lords. Therefore, I am glad when they say to me, let us go into the house of the Lord because in Your presence is fullness of joy. (Psalm 16: 11). There is joy because You love me and You are always with me.

You are my Shepherd; You take care of me both day and night. When Satan attacks me, You lift up a standard against him. You are an awesome and powerful God. When I am attacked, I know the battle is not mine, but the battle is Yours. The Word of God states, vengeance is the Lord's. (Romans 12:19). Therefore, I shout with the voice of triumph by Christ Jesus.

Thank You, Father, for giving Your son Jesus, to pay the price for my sins so that by my faith I am saved and justified (just as if I'd never sinned).

Thank You, Lord Most High, for peace that passes all understanding regardless to circumstances. You heal me whenever I am sick. You are my Provider. You provide all my needs. Father, You are my source of every good and every perfect gift. With a heart of gratitude, I say thank You.

This day I speak bountiful spiritual, physical, emotional, financial and relational blessings over me and the people of God through Jesus Christ. I love You, Lord, with all my heart, mind, soul, and strength in Jesus' name. Amen.

NEVER ALONE

SCRIPTURE REFERENCE

Psalm 68:6

*6)   God sets the solitary (lonely) in families; He brings out those who
are bound into prosperity...*

PRAYER

Father God, thank You for my spiritual family as well as my
natural family. Thank You for my church where the Bible based,
divine Word of God is taught. It is when I assemble myself with
others in the House of God, I experienced the love and joy of God
and my spiritual family.

Father, whenever I feel lonely, the Holy Spirit within me
reminds me that You said You will never leave me nor forsake me,
and I am comforted by the fact I am never alone because you are
always with me.

Thank You God, for prospering me with joy in the Lord Jesus,
with peace that passes all understanding, with mercy, with favor,
with all my needs met, and for delivering me from evil.

Father God, I thank You for 1) loving me, 2) calling me your
beloved, 3) calling me a child of God and 4) for making me joint
heir with your son, Jesus Christ. Lord, I am truly blessed. It is with
love, thanksgiving and gratitude, I pray in the precious name of
Jesus. Amen.

The Lord's Benefits

Scripture Reference

Psalm 68:19

19) *Blessed be the Lord, who daily loads us with benefits, the God of our salvation. Selah.*

Prayer

Father, thank You for the many benefits You provide. Thank You for the air to breathe, food to eat, water to drink, close to wear, shelter, eyes to see, ears to hear, a voice to talk, legs to walk, and a sound mind. Lord, You are the source of all my blessings. Each day I enjoy the favor you have placed on my life. You are my peace and hope. Father, thank You for Your mercy, grace, kindness, and most of all Your unconditional love.

Thank You Father for the greatest benefit you have given me, which is to save me from darkness and to bring me into Your marvelous light. Heaven is now my home where I shall live eternally. To You, God, be the glory, the honor, and the praise forever in Jesus' name. Amen.

The Lord's Benefit

Scripture Reference

Psalm 84:11

11) *For the Lord God is a sun and shield; The Lord will give grace and glory; no good thing will he withhold from those who walk uprightly.*

Prayer

Lord God, I thank You for being my sun that illuminates and guides me in the way I should go. I thank You for being my shield from harm and danger.

Father, when I am in pain, You heal me. When I am broken-hearted, You comfort me and give me peace. When I have a financial need, You meet my needs. When friends disappoint me, Your friendship sustains me. When Satan attacks me, You give me strength and the power to be, to be victorious. When I sin or miss the mark, You forgive me.

Father, thank You for good and perfect gifts. Thank You for favor with God and man, Lord, I want to walk uprightly according to Your Word and according to: Your way, Your will, Your spirit, and Your plan for my life, (to which I say yes) and according to the purpose for which You created me. Father, I say yes to the desires You placed in my heart. My trust is in You. Heavenly Father, I love You and I pray in the precious name of Jesus. Amen.

187

LOVE OUR CREATOR

SCRIPTURE REFERENCE

Psalm 100:2a -3

2a)   *Serve the Lord with gladness...*

3)   *Know that the Lord, He is God; It is He who has made us and not we ourselves. We are His people and the sheep of His pasture.*

PRAYER

Lord, I know You are God; above You there is none other. You are the one and only God. You are God who created me and all humanity. I serve You with gladness, because I am your child. I am among those who are called the people of God and I am a joint heir with Your son, Jesus Christ.

Father, thank You for being my Shepherd who takes care of me, who watches over me, who protects me, and who provides everything I need.

Lord, I serve You with gladness. Father, I am eternally grateful for Your goodness, Your mercy, Your grace, Your blessings and Your unconditional love. Lord, protect and bless my family and all the people of God. I pray in the name of Jesus. Amen.

REDEEMED

SCRIPTURE REFERENCE

Psalm 107:1, 2

1) *Oh, give thanks to the Lord, for He is good! For His mercy endures forever.*

2) *Let the redeemed of the Lord say so, whom He has redeemed from the hand of the enemy.*

PRAYER

Lord, I acknowledge, declared and proclaim my redemption. Because I am redeemed, I know, no matter how things appear, I have the victory in Christ Jesus.

Father, I revere You and thank You for deploring angels to encamp around me to protect me from the attacks of the enemy. I thank You and give You the highest praise for You are good and Your mercy endures forever. Thank You for redeeming me from Satan and bringing me into Your marvelous light.

Father, I worship You and give You the highest praise for You are worthy of all the praise, honor and glory in the precious name of Your Son Jesus Christ I pray. Amen.

GIVE THANKS

SCRIPTURE REFERENCE

Psalm 107:8

8)   *Oh, that men would give thanks to the Lord for His goodness and for His wonderful works to the children of men!*

PRAYER

Father, I give You thanks for Your goodness and Your wonderful works in my life. Father, I thank You for allowing me to see another day, a day that You have made, I shall rejoice and be exceedingly glad in it; for this I say thank You.

For health and strength. I say thank You. Lord I thank You for ordering my steps in the Word of God. You said, I am justified by my faith in Jesus. Therefore, I praise You for looking at me as if I never sinned because in Your sight I am covered by the blood of Jesus. Thank You Lord God.

I am grateful Lord, that You have begun a good work in me and You shall perform it until the day of Jesus Christ. I am grateful that You are the Author and the Finisher of my faith, and my latter days shall be greater than my former. Lord, I thank You for never leaving me nor forsaking me.

Father, I pray for the Holy Spirit to infuse my heart, body, and soul. I petitioned Him to empower me to be a doer of the Word and not a hearer only. I love You Lord and I thank You for Your love, mercy and grace. I pray in the awesome and precious name of Jesus. Amen.

DECLARE THE WORKS OF THE LORD

SCRIPTURE REFERENCE

Psalm 118:17

17) "I shall not die, but live, and declare the works of the Lord".

PRAYER

Lord, I want to live regardless to trouble, afflictions and pain and I declare Your works. I shall tell of Your works, Your grace, Your mercy, Your love, Your blessings, Your good works and Your perfect gifts.

I shall not die because I have not yet reached my God given potential. I have not yet completed the purpose for which I was created. You have destined me to do more for the Kingdom of God. Thank You for long life. I shall live and obey Your commands, declare Your works and glorify Your name all the days of my life. In Jesus' name Amen.

195

MY HELP

SCRIPTURE REFERENCE

Psalm 121:1, 2

1)   I will lift my eyes to the hills - from whence comes my help?

2)   My help comes from the Lord, Who made heaven and earth.

PRAYER

Lord, I lift up my eyes toward the sky as I thank You for Your never-ending help. Help me to remember scriptures in the Bible so that I may obey and please You in all I say, think and do; and I am able to share the Word of God with others. When I pray You help me; You answered my prayers.

When I enjoy the sunshine and the rain, I think of You. When I look at the trees and hear the birds sing. I think of You and praise Your holy name. Lord, when I look at flowers, the blue sky and the white clouds, I think of what an awesome God You are.

Father God, my help comes from You who made heaven and earth. You made me and all mankind. I thank You for my life and for promising me long life. I thank You for being my Help. Thank You for Your unconditional love and for who You are. In Jesus' name. Amen.

GOD IS PRESENT

SCRIPTURE REFERENCE

Psalm 139:7-10

7)   *Where can I go from Your Spirit? Or where can I flee from Your presence?*

8)   *If I ascend into heaven, You are there; If I make my bed in hell, behold You are there.*

9)   *If I take the wings of the morning and dwell in the uttermost parts of the sea,*

10) *even there Your hand shall lead me, and Your right hand shall hold me.*

PRAYER

Father, I am grateful that no matter where I go, You are always with me. You are omnipresent. You are in me, above me and all around me. I find great comfort in knowing You are always present. I am never alone. I feel Your presence and love deep in my heart. It is because Your hand holds me, I am protected. I am safe.

Thank You, Father, for leading me in the path of righteousness. Thank You for Your favor, Your mercy, Your good and perfect gifts and Your unconditional love. I love You and I give you all the glory, honor and praise in the precious name of Jesus. Amen.

199

PRAISE THE LORD

SCRIPTURE REFERENCE

Psalm 150:2,6

2) *Praise Him for His mighty acts; Praise Him according to His excellent greatness!*
6) *Let everything that has breath praise the Lord.*

PRAYER

Father, I praise You for Your mighty acts in my life: for waking me up this morning and giving me the desire to study the Word of God. I praise You for protecting me from harm and danger. Father, I acknowledged that in the midst of trouble, only You can give me peace. Mighty is Your act of providing those things I have need of. I praise You for opening doors of opportunity and for making my latter days better than my former.

Father, I believe and receive the miracles that are forthcoming in my life. I praise You for blessings and miracles in my life, and in my relationships. I thank You for health and financial blessings. Father, I rebuked the attacks of Satan, and ask You almighty God to continue to rebuke Satan on my behalf.

Lord, as You place those who need to be encouraged on my heart, I will be careful to reach out to them and without delay I will pray. I know, prayer changes things. Father, I continue to offer You the sacrifice of praise for Your never-ending love for me. So, it is with the great love that I say thank You. In Jesus' name. Amen.

WORSHIP GOD

SCRIPTURE REFERENCE

Revelations 7:11-12

11) *All the angels stood around the throne and the elders and the four living creatures, and fell on their faces before the throne and worshiped God,*

12) *saying: "Amen! Blessing and glory and wisdom, thanksgiving and honor and power and might, be to our God forever and ever. Amen."*

PRAYER

Father, I worship You for who You are. You are the mighty and powerful God. Because of Your power, Father, I know that when I am filled with Your spirit, I am empowered. So I ask You to fill me with Your Holy Spirit, that I may have strength and power to obey Your commands and do Your will on earth as it is in heaven.

Father, I give You all the honor and praise for You are worthy to be praised. Father, help me to honor You through my testimony, through my ministry and through my works because as the inspired Word of God, (the Holy Bible) says, faith without works is dead. Lord, order my steps in Your Word. Help me to honor You through my thoughts, my words, my spirit, my emotions, my choices, my behavior, and my actions.

Lord You are my ever-present Help in times of trouble. You are full of love and infinite wisdom. The Bible tells me in James 1:5 if anyone lacks wisdom, let him ask of God and it will be given him. Father, I ask You for divine wisdom in all I say and do. I ask for wisdom in relationships, wisdom in my home, wisdom with my finances, and wisdom in every facet of my daily life.

I pray that Your will be done in me and through me. I pray that Your will be done on earth as it is in Heaven.

Dear God, I experience Your love and kindness each day, so I say thank You. Thank You for every good gift and every perfect gift that comes down from You the Father of light, my Heavenly Father. Thank You for air to breath, eyes to see, ears to hear, a voice to speak, to pray, to praise and for hands to lift up without wrath and doubting. Father, I join the Angels in saying: blessing, glory, wisdom, thanksgiving, honor, power, and might be to God forever and ever. It is in Jesus' name I pray. Amen.

203

GOD THE CREATOR

SCRIPTURE REFERENCE

Revelation 4:11

11) *You are worthy. Oh Lord, to receive glory and honor and power; for You created all things, and by Your will they existed and were created.*

PRAYER

Lord, I was created to give You glory and honor. You are worthy to receive my heartfelt praise because of who You are. You are the Alpha and the Omega, the First and the Last the Beginning and the End.

You are the sovereign and eternal God. You are everything to me. For who You are. I give You glory, honor and praise.

Lord, You are Jehovah Jireh, my Provider. Just as You provided Abraham a ram in the thicket, You provide me shelter, the food I eat, the clothes I wear and the air I breathe. For who You are, I glorify Your name.

Lord, You are Jehovah Rapha, my Healer. Thank You for healing me every time I am sick. Father, You are Jehovah Nissi, my banner because of who You are in my life, I have victory over my enemy, the devil. So, I say thank You Lord. You are Jehovah Rohi, my shepherd. You take care of me, watch over me, protect me, and feed me with the Word of God and I am grateful. Father, thank You for Your mercy, grace and love. In the precious name of Jesus. Amen.

JUSTIFIED

SCRIPTURE REFERENCE

Romans 2:13

13)   For not the hearers of the law are just in the sight of God, but the doers of the law will be justified.

PRAYER

Lord, I enter Your gates with thanksgiving and Your courts with praise. Father, I do not want to be just a hearer of Your Word, I want to be a doer of Your Word. Help me to live according to Your will and not my own. Lord, thank You for the Holy Spirit who gives me the power to resist the devil and the lust of the flesh.

Dear God, I thank You for life. I thank You for health, for wholeness, for a sound mind and for peace that passes all understanding.

Father, I thank You for my family and friends, but most of all I thank You for Jesus who paid the price for my sins with His own blood. Now I know, that because I have accepted Jesus as my Lord and Savior, I am saved. So, I say thank You. Father, not only do I decree I am a doer of Your will, but I worship and love You with my whole heart, mind, soul, and strength. It is in Jesus' name I pray, Amen.

JUSTIFIED

SCRIPTURE REFERENCE

Romans 5:8, 9

8)   *But God demonstrates His own love toward us, in that while we were still sinners, Christ died for us.*

9)   *Much more then, having now been justified by His blood, we shall be saved from wrath through Him.*

PRAYER

Heavenly Father, I am grateful to Your son Jesus, for loving me and shedding His own blood for my sins. It is because I believe in Jesus, I am vindicated, just as if I never sinned. So I say thank You.

Father, I know I am an overcomer and I have victory over Satan by the blood of Jesus and the word of my testimony.

Lord, I am committed to pleasing You and to letting Your will be done in my life. Father, I ask You to fill me with the knowledge of Your will. Dear God, I want my life to fully pleased You. I asked You to empower me through the Holy Spirit to please You in all I say, all I think and in all I do. Order my steps in Your word. Let Your will be done in me, to me, and through me.

Dear God, I thank You for Your presence in me, and for permitting me to feel Your presence. Almighty God, continue to bless me and all the people of God. I love You Lord and praise You for who You are. In the precious name of Jesus', I pray, Amen.

OUR HOPE

Romans 15:13

13) *May God, the source of hope, fill you with all joy and peace by means of your faith in Him, so that your hope will continue to grow by the power of the Holy Spirit.*

PRAYER

Father God, You are my source of hope. You are my source of peace and joy, because my faith is in You. My faith is not in my possessions, nor my career, nor in the size of my bank account. Heavenly Father, my faith is in You which continues to grow by the power of the Holy Spirit, who is my Comforter. I thank You that I can do all things through Christ who strengthens me.

Dear God, by my faith, please continue to fill me with hope, joy, and peace as I let Your will be done in my life. In all that I do, I shall acknowledge You and give You all the glory, honor and praise. In Jesus' name. Amen.

211

OUR HOPE

SCRIPTURE REFERENCE

Psalm 130:5

5)   I wait for the Lord; my soul waits, and in His Word, I do hope.

PRAYER

Lord, my hope is in You. My hope is in the promises You made in Your Word, the Holy Bible. I hold fast to my hope and wait patiently on Your will to be done in my life.

Lord, You are my hope because of who You are and because You supply all my needs according to Your riches in glory. You own the cattle on a thousand hills. You are the Possessor of heaven and earth, and You give me good and perfect gifts. Thank You Father.

Father, though I am weak, I say I am strong because in my weakness You become my strength. Lord, increase the love, loyalty and harmony in my family and in my relationships. Father, it is my desire to serve the purpose for which You created me. Therefore, I ask that You give me the desire, understanding, wisdom, opportunity, and passion to serve in the areas You ordained for me before the foundation of the world. I love and thank You for loving me. In the name of Jesus, I pray. Amen.

213

THE GRACE IN JESUS

SCRIPTURE REFERENCE

Timothy 2:1, 3

1) *You therefore, my son, be strong in the grace that is in Christ Jesus.*
3) *You therefore must endure hardship as a good soldier of Jesus Christ.*

PRAYER

Lord, thank You for Your grace, which gives me strength to be what You want me to be and to do what you want me to do.

In times of hardship, I am reminded that You God, are my helper. You help me to overcome psychological and emotional pain. Psalm 34:19 states, "Many are the afflictions of the righteous, but the Lord delivers him out of them all".

Lord, You are my Banner of victory over all circumstances. You are God my Shepherd who takes care of me. You are my Healer who heals me whenever I am sick. You are my Peace regardless to the circumstances. You are my Provider. You provide my needs, and every good and every perfect gift.

Thank You Father, as it is stated in John 16:33… "in the world, you will have tribulations: but be of good cheer; I have overcome the world". Father, thank You for favor and strength in times of hardship and tribulations, I shall be of good cheer because all power is in Your hand and I am in Your hands. You are my Father who loves me, and I am Your child who loves You. Father, I thank You and praise You for who You are in the name of Jesus. Amen.

GOD INSPIRED SCRIPTURES

SCRIPTURE REFERENCE

Timothy 3:16

16) All scripture is given by inspiration of God, and is profitable for doctrine, for reproof, for correction, for instruction in righteousness.

PRAYER

Father God, I thank You for Your doctrine. Thank You for reproof, correction, and instruction. I know scriptures in the Holy Bible were inspired by You, my Heavenly Father. Father, I am diligent to use the Bible as my instruction manual for righteous living. I shall obey Your Word which equips me for every good and godly work. The scriptures teach me how to be righteous, that is to be in right standing with God through Jesus Christ.

Father, I want to obey You, I want to please You in all I do, say and think. As I study Your Word, if I discover there is need for me to change something in my life, I shall make the change. It is my desire each day to be more Christ-like.

Dear God, I thank You for Your abundant blessings, mercy, protection, favor and love. In Jesus' name I pray, Amen.

217

Meditate, Continually Think and Speak the Following Scriptures

1 Corinthians 13: 13

And now abide, faith, hope, love, these three, but the greatest of these is love.

2 Corinthians 12:9

And he said to me, MY grace is sufficient for you, for My strength is made perfect in weakness.

Deuteronomy 6:5

You shall love the Lord your God with all your heart, with all your soul, and with all your strength.

Jeremiah 29:11

For I know the thoughts that I think toward you, says the Lord, thoughts of peace and not of evil, to give you a future and a hope.

John 14:15

If you love Me, keep My commandments.

John 15:12

This is My commandment, that you love one another as I have loved you.

1 John 4:8

He who does not love does not know God, for God is love.

Luke 18:27

But He said, "The things which are impossible with men are possible with God".

Philippians 4:13

I can do all things through Christ who strengthens me.

Philippians 4:19

And my God shall supply all your need according to His riches in glory by Christ Jesus.

Psalm 119:105

Your word is a lamp to my feet and a light to my path.

Romans 8:37b

… we are more than conquerors through him (Jesus) who loved us.

2 Timothy 1:7

for God has not given us a spirit of fear, but of power and of love and of a sound mind.

Praise Old Testament

2 Chronicles 7:6b

…with instruments of music of the Lord, which King David had made to praise the Lord, saying, "For His mercy endures forever"

Daniel 2:23

I thank You and praise You, O God of my fathers; You have given me wisdom and might...

Deuteronomy 10:21

Praise Him "He is your praise, and He is your God, who has done for you these great and awesome things which your eyes have seen".

Exodus 15:2

The Lord is my strength and song, and He has become my salvation; He is my God and I will praise Him; my father's God and I will exalt Him.

Isaiah 63:7

I will mention the lovingkindness of the Lord, And the praises of the Lord, according to all the Lord has bestowed on us...

Psalm 7:17

I will praise the Lord according to H2is righteousness and will sing praise to the name of the Lord Most High.

Psalm 28:7

The Lord is my strength and my shield; my heart trusted in Him and I am help; therefore my heart greatly rejoice, and with my song I will praise Him.

Forgiving

As we take a look at forgiving and forgiveness, we are reminded that receiving forgiveness from God depends on if we forgive others. Jesus Christ forgave those who crucified Him; those who beat Him, spat on Him, pierced Him in his side and nail Him to the cross, causing Him to die a shameful death. Yet, He said "forgive them for they know not what they do". No human being has suffered as much as Jesus. Therefore, as children of God, we must forgive all those who offend us and all those who sin against us.

Matthew 6:14-15 NLT

If you forgive those who sin against you, your heavenly Father will forgive you, but if you refuse to forgive others, your Father will not forgive your sins".

Pray

Lord, You forgave me all of my sins and as your child, I shall forgive those who sin against me. It is when I forgive those who sin against me, You forgive me, but if I do not forgive them, You will not forgive me of my sins.

Luke 6:37

Do not judge and you will not be judged. Do not condemn and you will not be condemned. Forgive and you will be forgiven.

Pray

Father God, I shall not judge nor condemn others, I shall forgive them as You Heavenly Father have forgiven me.

About the Author

REVEREND CLARICE BELL Church is a retired educator and entrepreneur. She is a native of Atlanta Georgia where she received her bachelor's degree from Spellman College, her master's degree from Clark Atlanta University and Doctor of Ministry Degree from Beacon University. Currently Reverend Church is an associate Elder at Word of Faith Family Worship Cathedral in metro Atlanta where Bishop Dale C. Bronner is the Founder and Senior Pastor. Reverend Church over the years has dedicated much of her life to following God's plan for her life as a prayer warrior standing in the gap for God's people. Reverend Church believes Bible-based Prayers and Praise is not just a book for her it is truly a way of life and prays it becomes that for you as well.

Made in the USA
Columbia, SC
17 November 2018